# FAT MAN IN THE
# KITCHEN

# FAT MAN IN THE KITCHEN

TOM VERNON

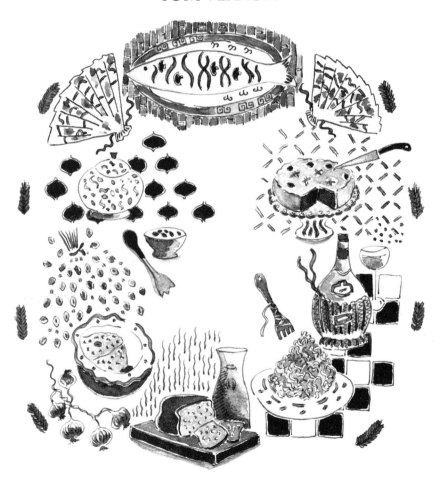

BBC PUBLICATIONS

To aunt Marian

'The discovery of a new dish does more for the happiness of
mankind than the discovery of a star.' Brillat-Savarin

Published by BBC Publications.
A division of BBC Enterprises Ltd,
35 Marylebone High Street,
London W1M 4AA

First published 1986
Reprinted 1986

ISBN 0 563 20464 8 (paperback)
0 563 204621 (hardback)

Colour Plates printed by
Chorley and Pickersgill Ltd, Leeds

Typeset in 11/13 Palatino

Printed and bound in Great Britain by
Butler & Tanner, Frome and London

# CONTENTS

# INTRODUCTION: THE GLOBAL KITCHEN

We are entering the age of the global kitchen. We know about fresh sardines because we have eaten them on holiday; tropical fruit comes in by plane; television shows another nation eating something strange and, like a child watching another with a chocolate bar, we want the same.

The global kitchen is not an international kitchen which reduces everything to a norm of acceptability, the standard fare of the hotel chains in which every room air-conditions your prejudices and keeps you away from the reality of the country outside. The global kitchen is all kitchens to all men and women.

The most important change is still to come: that all kitchens on the globe are supplied with food; but it will come. It is inconceivable that people who do not like to be hungry themselves can see starvation on the screen in their own dining rooms for ever, and not exert some influence on their politicians. People cannot afford to remain ignorant unless they live in a small, simple society. You can stay stupid in a village, but if you take your stupidity to the town, the traffic runs you over. As well as a morality of nutrition, we will need a global philosophy of cooking in our global kitchen. Already, those who stipulate steak pie and chips in lands of salads and garlic are figures of fun. Even the French, marvellous as their food is, are going to have to give up some of their chauvinism.

There are not many areas in which Britain is in the culinary forefront, but, as it happens, we are one of the countries which has always had a global kitchen. As a sea-going and exploring nation, we have been pinching other people's recipes for centuries, and adapting them to suit ourselves: more recently, immigration has brought us exciting shops and restaurants. An ability to plunder is not something to be particularly proud of, of course, but to take an idea from another country is often the opposite of imperialism – a sign of respect or friendship.

Looking out across the world from my homemade kitchen in Muswell Hill has brought me not only recipes but an occasional will o' the wisp of understanding. It is like going up on a hill to see a landscape – instead of a hedgerow, you see a boundary; instead of a road, a link. This book offers you my view.

I have tried to think about recipes in relation to the life of the country; and this has sometimes led me into personal opinions – which are not the responsibility of the BBC. A cookery book is not the place to set the world to rights, but it is not the place to ignore it, either. My cat, Zaiki, does not care about the happiness of mice, men, or other small animals: that is quite OK for cats, but not for cooks, whose role in life is to give satisfaction, and to be continually creative.

Though some of the chefs in the television series were outstanding, many of the cooks were quite humble people. It was a democratic series, and unusually international: cooks and broadcasters of each country chose the recipes they would like to show to the rest of the world, and made programmes about them more or less to an agreed format. Then each member of the club gave their programmes to everybody else.

So my first acknowledgement is to cooks great and small throughout the world; to the broadcasting organisations who made the programmes – and to those involved in the British editions made by the BBC at Manchester: Cyril Gates (producer), Sue Lochead (director), Roger Bolton, Colin Adams, Cathy Broderick, Judi Rose and, particularly, Rachel Grisewood and Jo Christian. Various other forms of support came from Sally Vernon, Leolinda Costa, Alistair Wilson, Sally Jones, Jos Vernon, Allen Smith, Carol Haslam, Jenny De Yong, Sandra Harvey, Jeremy Eccles, Madeleine Kállay-Tomalin, Alison Leeming, Jenny Wilford, Joan Morgan, Roy Grove of the Snail Centre, Colwyn Bay, and from the German Food Centre, the Swedish Delicatessen and the tourist offices, trade commissions and embassies of all countries. Finally, no one can write a recipe book without thinking of the way their mother used to cook; and I haven't.

*Tom Vernon*

# EXPLANATIONS

The recipes were originally tested by the various cooks who were filmed in each country: but translation often produced instructions which were about as clear as chocolate mousse, and frequently contradictory. The writing of this book to a particularly tight schedule has only allowed me to test a few of the recipes myself before the print deadline, but to this has been added the professional work of the home economists Rachel Grisewood and Judi Rose, who worked on the British television programmes, and that of Jo Christian, who sieved and strained the copy for the book. I have done my best to clarify and correct (hoping that by doing so I introduced no additional errors). But because the recipes come from many different people, as well as many different countries, the style of cooking sometimes varies, and occasional idiosyncrasies come through the BBC's housestyle.

*Bain-marie* People with frivolous minds like mine will want to know who Marie was. It is said that she was a fourth-century Jewish alchemist, and that the first bain-marie maintained its constant temperature with heated sand, not water. I don't think that has much to do with cooking, but it gives me an excuse to mention the man who said it, the Victorian journalist E. S. Dallas, who wrote the marvellous *Kettner's Book of the Table*, which you ought to read. Oh, and by the way, it is a water bath to moderate heat and spread it evenly – any suitably shaped pan with water in it will do: stand the food in a bowl in or above the water so that it cooks gradually and evenly. The method is particularly useful for preparing egg-based sauces or custards which would spoil if heated too fiercely.

*Clarified butter* Clarified butter (*ghee*) is useful in everyday cooking and, I think, indispensable for curries and the like, where it gives a rich flavour without causing a holocaust of burnt spices on the bottom of the pan. Butter is rather more than four-fifths fat and one-fifth water, salt, casein and lactose, which burn at quite a low temperature. Adding a little oil makes it possible to fry hotter, but clarifying the butter removes the problem entirely, and also makes it possible to keep the butter for a long time – a year, in a cool place. When you melt butter, the residues go two ways – sink to the bottom and foam to the top. I find that the easiest way to clarify butter is to melt it and cook it at a low heat for a few minutes to ensure that the clear golden fat is well separated out, skim off the foam from the top, then pour the butter off from the residues through a paper towel. (Vegetable *ghee* can be made from margarine in the same way; and those who are unable to tell the difference will be unable to tell the difference.) Another method is to stir the hot butter to encourage the scum to sink to the bottom, refrigerate, and spoon off the solidified *ghee* from the top. Yet another method is to cook the butter in such a way that the solids stick to the bottom of the pan without burning too badly.

*Herbs* Thyme, rosemary and marjoram/oregano are among the herbs which dry quite well. With more delicate herbs, however, it is often better to change the herb rather than use a dried one: I give little credit to dried tarragon, none at all to dried parsley – and dried basil, in particular, is a pathetic wraith of its aromatic self. Keeping basil under oil flavours the oil, but reduces the leaves to slimy black things which look as if they have come from the bottom of a particularly nasty pond. If you grow your own herbs, freeze them. There is no need to go through the palaver of embedding them in ice cubes, washings, dryings and other things sometimes recommended. Take them off the plant on a sunny day, put them in a bag and put the bag in the freezer – that is all.

*Pepper* In this book pepper is any colour you like so long as it is black, and freshly ground. Where white pepper is preferable (notably in Chinese cooking), it is specified in the recipe.

*Shrimps (or prawns)* Cleaning shrimps and prawns is an individual matter, depending on the relationship between you and the shrimp. Some are so small you would go crazy trying; bigger ones have an obvious intestinal tract which only people who are quite easy-going about such things will not want to remove ('de-veining' is the euphemism). Shrimps are scavengers and less pernickety about their food than you are: some people who are susceptible to shellfish poisoning may happily eat a cleaned prawn, but be tied up in knots by a more casually treated one. Raw prawns can be very difficult to find: in their absence, you have to take what you can get – and afford.

*Stock* Stock cubes are very useful, but not the same as good stock which you make yourself. They offer nowhere near the variety or quality – the glutinous smoothness of veal, the richness of game, the strength of beef. If you do use cubes, be sparing. If you use too many, the artificiality of the taste is very noticeable – and well nigh impossible to get rid of.

*Shallots* I have come across a tendency to call a spring onion a shallot. While you can have a young shoot of shallot, just like a spring onion (both are known as scallions, which may be where the confusion originates), in this book a shallot is a dry shallot. Its main advantage is that it has a penetrating taste with a hint of garlic, which allows you to flavour a dish with less bulk and water than is contributed by a large onion.

*Soured cream* Soured cream, as found all over Northern Europe, is a culture, not quite the same as ordinary cream with lemon juice added, but fairly similar. If you can't get soured cream, add a teaspoon of lemon to 150 ml ($\frac{1}{4}$ pint) of single or double cream and leave it to thicken for half an hour. *Crème fraîche* is matured cream with a slight sourish quality.

*Weights and measures* The measures given in recipes are based on those of the country of origin; and, as in most practical things, translating from one system to another can produce some rather odd results – or, in this case, fractions. It is sometimes sensible to round up or down, and sometimes less so. You should not need to worry about apparent inconsistencies.

*Woks* The wok is one of the most useful and versatile pieces of kitchen equipment ever invented. The temperature graduates as you go up the sides, making it possible to cook at several heats at once; and as well as being invaluable for stir-frying, it can also be used to steam (with its lid on) and to deep-fry. When a wok is full of boiling water or hot fat, it is *vital* to make sure that it is well supported: a wok-ful of boiling oil can easily produce injuries which Vlad the Impaler would classify as thoroughly entertaining. (This danger is less in many Chinese kitchens, where the wok sits in a hole in the top of the cooker.) To steam in a wok, rest a plate or grill rack across a pair of chopsticks half-way up. Using this sort of support you can also smoke food, though whatever you heat at the bottom will need to be in small pieces – you could use tea leaves, for example.

*Yeast* Yeast may be fresh or dried, and dried yeast is available both in granular form and as a powder. Weight for weight, you need to use only half as much dried as fresh yeast. Each of the three forms of yeast needs slightly different preparation. Dried granules should be put with a little warm water in a bowl and left for ten minutes or so, until the granules have broken up and the liquid has become slightly frothy. Fresh yeast is just creamed with warm water and added to the flour straightaway. Powdered yeast is simply sprinkled straight into the flour, before adding water.

# ONE PLACE LIKE HOME
## AUSTRALIA

'5.30–6.45 *Monday to Saturday: Rump Steak $4, T-bone Steak $4*' Menu at Hughenden
Refreshment Rooms, quoted in Scyld Berry's *Train to Julia Creek*

The British tend to have a rather confused view of Australia. They think of
Australia as one of the family – that is, they think it looks familiar. On the
other hand, they have a folk memory of a place to which the package tours
go in chains; and they cannot escape the thought that it has to be a hard life
in the land of billabongs and kangaroo-tail soup. When it comes to Australian
cooking, they may have heard of the internationally famous meat pie and
tomato ketchup – which a Japanese airline is said to have served to the luxury
class on the Australian run under the impression that it was the Aussie national
dish. Those particular British and Japanese impressions are crook. The average
Australian home has no leg-irons and no kangaroo. And tucker is bonzer down
there.

Being so huge, and being an island as well, gives Australia a highly varied
climate which is, however, temperate in enough of the right places; and what
this means to the cook is melons, pawpaws, pineapples, bananas and passion
fruit all year round. There are few vegetables that remember what it's like to
be out of season; though there is also the dried fruit we put in our cakes. The
land flows with meat and honey. People can actually afford the best cuts of
high-quality beef and lamb. Australian bees are tycoons among bees – they
make more per hive than any others in the world. The seas are full of food –
oysters, abalone, tunny, lobsters, scallops, squid and octopus as well as
creatures humbler and even more exotic – or dangerous.

Having begun as a land of leg-irons, Australia has developed an enthusiasm
for liberty and a distrust of authority. And it was Australia that coined one of

the great words of the English language – 'wowser', a kill-joy, after those who cry, self-righteously, 'We Only Want the Rectification of Social Evils'. Kill-joys are no use in a kitchen, where success depends on a love of creation, and of Creation. (Little children, never waste your cooking on a wowser. Reformers, yes, wowsers no. They are happier with sandwiches.) Independence is a good thing in cooks whose age-old cry is '*My* Kitchen' and Australians have a good deal of space to be independent in.

There is scrub and desert to spare, with the Northern Territory dry enough for camels all the way to Alice Springs and the 'dead heart' of the continent beyond; and the inland vastness of Western Australia, where it may be fifty miles across a red-soil plain to get the beer. Where sheep and acres alike run in thousands and the only tourist boom ever known was the gold-rush, there are few graces, but the kind of good-fellowship that comes from not having many fellows.

The days of the cowboy cattle-drovers are not gone. They are no longer overlanders, travelling from one end of the country to the other, but stockmen out in the bush for weeks, whipping their way to market for days on end, driving the herd dustily before them. They still have a camp-fire cookery which is a matter of necessity, not playing boy scouts. The billy-can, for tea, is one of the world's humblest utensils, being no more than a jumped-up paint tin hung over the fire, guaranteed to scald and burn. The other basic implement, in contrast, is a splendid cast-iron pot with three little legs, a good lid and a handle. Hung over the fire, it is a cauldron for Camp Soup, an open-air stew of extremely variable recipe; put into a hole in the ground with hot ashes from a good fire, it is an oven for Damper, baking powder bread – a gigantic, golden, crusty, crumbly scone to be attacked immediately it comes out of the ground with lots of butter and sugar-cane syrup. (It is a typically odd fact of human existence that Damper is only made where it is extremely dry.)

But this is no longer the typical Australia. Far from chasing sheep in the outback, with corks bobbing from their hats to keep off the flies, Australians today live in cities in well-to-do suburbia. Members of an urban society cannot wear bush hats to the office: they get in the way in the lifts. The new Australia has money, the energy of a young country, lots of good things to cook with, a European heritage that is rather distant and a Polynesian influence that is much closer to hand. The result is a cuisine that is lively, anarchic in its variety, sometimes apt to overdo it. Good food is rather young there, and behaves like it.

Until the 1950s and 1960s Australia was extraordinary in being a wine-making country that was not a wine-drinking country. The Australians were a nation of beer-guzzlers. They still are, but wine consumption quadrupled in the twenty years between 1962 and 1982. (Moderation is important in cooking, but countries with strong temperance movements do not eat well: you need relaxation and tolerance.) Wine-drinking grew with the waves of immigrants, mostly from Europe, who came down upon Australia like surfers on Bondi beach in the years after the Second World War. The immigrants brought other new tastes as well. Untied from the skirts of the British Empire, Australia began to look around her and feel that she mattered in the world; with greater prosperity and increasing city-dwelling, Australians began to eat out in Chinese, Indonesian or French; on Greek food, Hungarian food, Japanese food. And all made by Australians.

# AUSTRALIA

## SYDNEY, NEW SOUTH WALES

*'Land will be granted with a clause that will ever prevent more than one house being built on the allotment, which will be 60 feet in front and 150 feet in depth.'* Governor Phillip

Not everything about Sydney is as beautiful as the curving harbour and bays, blue water with green islands. The suburban spread is bigger than Greater London, with commuting journeys of an hour, bad-tempered traffic and all the rest of the urbanities of big-city life. You may not take to some of the local inhabitants: you swim behind wire netting, because of the sharks, root with some care in the rubbish for fear of the deadly red-back spider.

So, Sydney is not all marvellous: the other problem with it is that there can be as many as twenty-three days in the year when the sun does not shine.

It is a prosperous, lively, cosmopolitan place with a rough-and-ready past and great natural advantages, and the food reflects all this. In Sydney the delicatessens rival those of Soho – at least. Eating out nowadays, there is not much in the world of cooking that you cannot get, including sophistication; but the simplicity – even crudity – of a pioneering people stepping up into affluence is still visible. There is local nostalgia for the old tiled bars, swilling shops which were hosed down after hours as if they were public lavatories. The legendary Doyle's on the harbour is appreciated as much for the sauce of its waiters as for the quality of its seafood. Like London East Enders, Sydneysiders eat boiled shrimps out of paper bags. Here, though, is something very different: a dish of prawns that combines a Mediterranean quantity of garlic with Asian stir-frying – though it begins almost like a meringue.

# GARLIC PRAWNS WITH SHERRY

JOE DUARTE, DOYLE'S RESTAURANT, SYDNEY

ENOUGH FOR 4 TO 6 PEOPLE

| |
|---|
| **800 g (1$\frac{3}{4}$ lb) raw prawns, peeled and de-veined as necessary** |
| **1 egg white** |
| **2 teaspoons lemon juice** |
| **3 tablespoons very dry sherry** |
| **$\frac{1}{2}$ teaspoon salt** |
| **1$\frac{1}{2}$ tablespoons cornflour** |
| **7 medium cloves of garlic, peeled** |
| **Oil for deep-frying** |
| **2 spring onions** |
| **$\frac{1}{2}$ teaspoon fresh ginger, finely chopped or grated** |
| **1 chilli, finely chopped** |
| **50 ml (2 fl oz) chicken stock** |
| **1 teaspoon sugar** |
| **$\frac{1}{2}$ teaspoon white pepper** |
| **$\frac{1}{2}$ tablespoon soy sauce** |
| **1 teaspoon chilli oil (see pp. 94–5) or olive oil** |
| *Garnish* |
| **Parsley** |
| **Lemon slices** |

PREPARATION: Beat the egg white until stiff and fold in the lemon juice, 1 tablespoon of the sherry, the salt and the cornflour. Stir in the prawns and leave them to marinate for 10 to 15 minutes.

Crush 1 clove of garlic and put it to heat in the deep-frying oil, keeping an eye on it so that you can take it out when it's brown. Chop the rest of the garlic very finely. Quarter the spring onions lengthways and cut them into 5 to 7 cm (2 to 3 inch) pieces. Mix the chopped garlic and the onions with the ginger and chilli. In a bowl, mix the chicken stock with the sugar, pepper, soy sauce, chilli oil and the rest of the sherry.

Take out the crushed clove of garlic and deep-fry the prawns, not too many at a time for fear of cooling the oil too much, and not for more than a minute, which should be enough to colour them. Drain them on paper towels.

Drain the garlic oil from the pan, leaving about a teaspoon behind. Reheat it and cook the garlic/spring onion/ginger/chilli mixture for a minute. Add the prawns and then the stock. Stirring all the time, bring everything to the boil. When it has boiled, serve hot, garnished with parsley and slices of lemon.

～ • ～

Native Sydney cooking is based on the same principle as British traditional – no mucking about with the best ingredients; and there is more than a touch of the home country in Carpet-bag Steak, which perpetuates one of the favourite flavours of Victorian England – steak with oysters. A Sydneysider may hate the Egg Shell (the opera house); he may be blasé about the Coat Hanger (the Sydney Harbour Bridge); but you will never get him to admit that there is much better in the world than a Sydney rock oyster.

To the north of Sydney, the Hawkesbury river is a natural barrier to suburbia's taking over the world. The water is cleaner there, and in a quiet bay where rocks are encrusted with oysters growing naturally, even more oysters grow artificially, to go on to the plate or into the steak and on the barbie (Australian for barbecue). Carpet-bag Steak is rather expensive for a British barbecue, but can be cheapened, in every sense of the word, by substituting rougher cuts of meat and using bacon instead of oysters.

# CARPET-BAG STEAK
## TOM SCHOOTS, SYDNEY COLLEGE OF CATERING STUDIES
### ENOUGH FOR 4 KEEN CARNIVORES

| |
|---|
| **4 fillet steaks, each a good 5 cm (2 inches) thick, and weighing about 350 g (12 oz)** |
| **12 oysters** |
| **1 or 2 cloves of garlic, finely chopped** |
| **2 tablespoons chopped parsley** |
| **Oil and butter for frying** |
| **175 g (6 oz) breadcrumbs** |
| **100 g (4 oz) mushrooms, finely chopped** |
| **1 egg** |
| **Rind of $\frac{1}{2}$ lemon, grated** |
| **Salt and pepper** |

PREPARATION: Trim the fat from the meat, and cut a pocket in the side of each steak big enough to take a good tablespoon of stuffing. Open the oysters with a short kitchen knife wriggled between the two halves of the shell, with the hand that holds the oyster protected by a cloth. Think of something else to do with the liquor – don't waste it. Beard the oysters if you feel keen, but you can get away without if you don't. Mix half the garlic with the parsley.

Fry the rest of the garlic lightly in oil. Add the breadcrumbs and fry till golden brown (which takes no time at all). Put them to one side.

Soften the mushrooms gently in a mixture of oil and butter for 2 or 3 minutes; add the oysters and continue cooking for a further 3 minutes. Stir over high heat for one minute more, then take the pan off the heat.

Beat the egg in a mixing bowl and add the lemon rind, the garlic and parsley, the breadcrumbs and the mushrooms and oysters, mixing everything well. Stuff each steak with about a tablespoon of the mixture. Close the opening, using toothpicks.

Salt and pepper the steaks and fry them in oil and butter, leaving the inside pink (about 3 minutes each side).

# QUEENSLAND

*'They arrived with hand guns and automatics, shooting down the pawpaws ...'* Hippy evicted by police, quoted in Scyld Berry's *Train to Julia Creek*

Along the top right-hand quarter of Australia lies the Coral Sea and the 1300 miles of the Great Barrier Reef, a submarine garden-city for all kinds of exotic sea-creatures. On land, the gardens, with their avocados, papayas and mangoes, are hardly less exotic. In Port Douglas, a routine motel breakfast is papaya, passion fruit, local banana and coconut garnished with scarlet frangipani that looks as if its ambition is to give up being a flower and turn itself into a dress for a night-club singer. In the evening, on the verandah, the more fortunate citizens of this humdrum paradise drink local orange and lime juice mixed with the dark rum of the nearby cane-fields.

However, this Garden of Eden can be rather oppressive to live in, and occasionally dangerous. The local creepy-crawlies and crocodiles flourish along with the passion fruit; the sun not only browns but burns. Queensland has been a byword for reactionary politics: at one point the police commissioner was driven to resign on principle after a particularly high-handed police raid on a seaside hippy colony, an affair known as 'The Bay of Pigs'. Of course, the hippies were all the sorrier to go because Queensland is a place where significant luxuries do grow on trees, and come out of the sea.

Take a middle-class family who are well-off enough to have a large garden, a verandah, and friends who wear cocktail dresses to sit upon it – the Bowdens.

Diana Bowden's main course for her dinner party is baked Red Emperor from the Barrier Reef, a fish of imperial size; but tropical eating relies heavily on cold food, salads and elaborate starters, and Diana's first course is hardly less regal than the fish. It begins humbly. She sends one of the daughters down to the wharf on her bike to pick up some banana prawns – so-called because a banana is only slightly bigger than they are (you could use shrimps or crab meat instead). Diana gets the other main ingredients even more casually, from the garden, for Avocado and Prawns in Ravigote Mayonnaise.

# AVOCADO AND PRAWNS IN RAVIGOTE MAYONNAISE
DIANA BOWDEN, PORT DOUGLAS, QUEENSLAND

ENOUGH FOR 4 PEOPLE

| |
|---|
| 2–4 tablespoons ravigote mayonnaise |
| 2 large avocados |
| Juice of 1 lemon |
| 2 teaspoons double cream |
| 1 teaspoon brandy |
| 150 g (5 oz) prawns, cooked, peeled, de-veined and chopped into chunks |
| *Garnish* |
| 2 tablespoons grated Emmenthal cheese |
| 2 eggs, hard-boiled |
| $\frac{1}{2}$ lemon, sliced |
| 1 tomato, sliced |
| Some sprigs of parsley |
| *Ravigote Mayonnaise* (makes about 275 ml/$\frac{1}{2}$ pint) |
| 150 ml ($\frac{1}{4}$ pint) oil (I prefer half and half olive oil and groundnut) |
| 1 large egg yolk |
| 1 spring onion, finely chopped |
| 50 ml (2 fl oz) tarragon vinegar |
| 50 ml (2 fl oz) white wine |
| 1 tablespoon capers |
| 1 tablespoon finely chopped chervil |
| 1 tablespoon chopped parsley |
| Salt and pepper |

PREPARATION: Make the mayonnaise in the usual way, beating the oil into the egg yolk little by little. Boil the chopped spring onion hard with the vinegar and wine until the liquid is reduced by half. When it is cool, mix in the capers and the chopped herbs, season with salt and pepper, and combine with the mayonnaise. Halve the avocados and scoop out the middles, leaving a rim of flesh all round. Squeeze lemon juice over the rim and the scooped-out avocado flesh, to prevent blackening.

Mash the avocado flesh, add the cream (with a little more lemon juice to thicken it), and mix. Stir in the ravigote mayonnaise, brandy and prawns. Pile the mixture into the avocado halves. It should be quite thick already, but refrigerate for half an hour to encourage it to set further. Garnish with grated Emmenthal cheese; slices of egg, lemon and tomato; and some sprigs of parsley.

I find the garnish over the top, myself; and have doubts about the brandy and cream. It may pass in paradise, but I would take a simpler approach in our less luxurious land. Good food and drink is like good company – you choose it, for the individual qualities of the ingredients, how they contrast, how they go together. Being too rich, or expensive, or showy can get in the way.

The Polynesian way with fish is very different – little more than fish, lime juice and coconut milk. In Fiji, across the Coral Sea from Queensland, the traditional welcome to a guest is the presentation of a coconut as a token of fertility. The coconut is a kind of vegetable supermarket. You can live in it, dress in it, eat it, drink it, get drunk on it and walk on it. It is wood for a house, fibre for the carpets, cloth to wear, coconut meat and coconut milk. It is palm salad from the crown of the tree, palm wine and the cup to drink it from. It even wears a smile. The nut has a comic face – two brown eyes and a little brown mouth, all open wide in perpetual astonishment – and that is why Spanish explorers gave it its name. 'Coco' is Spanish for 'clown'.

Coconut milk is the sweetish water found inside, enriched with the flesh around it. A Polynesian would begin by chopping the end off a green nut with a machete. But then, in a young nut, the flesh is so soft that it can easily be spooned out as a translucent jelly. This flesh – or the grated meat of older nuts – is added to the coconut water in a bowl, stirred to break it up a bit, and squeezed in a cloth to extract the milk.

In Britain, there is no need to find a young coconut and a hatchet. Equal amounts of desiccated coconut and hot water (or warm dairy milk) can produce coconut milk that is, for most purposes, as good as or better than any you can make from a coconut available over here. All you need do is blend and strain – and a couple of pinches of sugar restore the sweetness found in mature nuts (green nuts are less sweet). Coconut milk can be made thicker or thinner according to taste and purpose. Often, it might better be called coconut cream, since it behaves rather in the same way as the dairy product: for instance, it is apt to curdle when boiled. So if you cook with it, keep it below boiling point, or add it at the end as an enrichment.

Coconut milk is a possible salad dressing for cucumber; it can be used in cakes; and the flesh of fresh coconut can be steeped in salt water for a week, pressed dry, moistened again with fresh coconut milk and flavoured with chilli, lemon and onion to make a relish. Fish in lime and coconut milk is a classic dish that is classically simple, too. The fish need not be coral trout, snapper, barracuda or anything else exotic and impossible to get: any firm-fleshed fish that is not fatty will do. Haddock, for instance, is fine. But it should be fresh.

# FISH WITH LIME AND COCONUT MILK
## JANI LAWRENCE, QUEENSLAND
### ENOUGH FOR 4 PEOPLE

| |
|---|
| 700 g (1½ lb) fish, filleted and cut into chunks |
| 250 ml (9 fl oz) lime juice or lemon juice |
| salt and pepper |
| 250 ml (9 fl oz) coconut milk (fresh, tinned or made as above) |
| *Garnish* |
| Spring onions, sweet red peppers, chillies, all chopped |

PREPARATION: Put the fish chunks in a bowl and souse them very well in the lime juice. Season with salt and pepper. Work the fish gently with your fingers to make sure the juice gets everywhere. Soak for about three hours at warm room temperature, or overnight in the fridge.

Drain the marinade. The acid will have pickled the fish and turned it white. Press the fish gently in the sieve: this does two things at once – it helps the juice to go into the chunks and it removes the surplus. Toss the fish in the coconut milk with a colourful garnish of green and white spring onions, sweet red peppers and mild chillies. (If the only chillies you can get are ferocious, rub a cut chilli over the pieces of pepper instead.)

~~ • ~~

The principle is quite like that of an oil and vinegar salad dressing – lime for sharpness, coconut milk for smoothness – but uniquely fresh-tasting. Don't let the idea of raw fish scare you – the effect is much more as if it has been cooked – but if you want to start gradually, make a lemon and coconut dressing for cucumber salad first; or add thick coconut milk to a tropical fruit salad.

# MELBOURNE, VICTORIA

Weather is 'changeable' in Melbourne, say some; 'drizzly', say others. The life of the Great Indoors is lived here more enthusiastically than elsewhere in Australia: the city is into art, fashion, sophistication. It had pretensions almost from the start, when its comparatively respectable immigrants refused to allow convict ships to land. It is still the Boston of Australia, though with the usual Australian diversity of newcomers.

This sort of society produces restaurants that seek distinction of style, as well as of food: so Melbourne food is represented here by the work of two well-known chefs. The dishes are not economical, but the techniques are by no means out of the reach of the ordinary cook.

At the Paternoster restaurant, Ernst Stuhler crowns his sweet-trolley with tall ice sculptures and as a main course serves a pretty dish of beef and fruit, a mixture of sweet and savoury guaranteed to appeal to Australian taste. Beef Mildura is rather like a high-protein Swiss roll, and is even more colourful. It is named after a town on the Murray river in the far corner of Victoria. The fact that Mildura claims to have the longest bar in the southern hemisphere has no relevance to this dish; but the town is also famous for its fruit.

# BEEF MILDURA
### ERNST STUHLER, PATERNOSTER RESTAURANT, MELBOURNE
### ENOUGH FOR 6 TO 8 PEOPLE

| 1 long fillet of beef, weighing about 1·5 kg ($3\frac{1}{4}$ lb) |
| --- |
| 25 g (1 oz) butter |
| Salt and white pepper |
| 4 to 6 slices of fat bacon, without rind |
| 1 peach |
| 1 firm avocado |
| 40 g ($1\frac{1}{2}$ oz) cornflour |

PREPARATION: Preheat the oven to 230°C (450°F, gas mark 8). Trim the steak, then cut it sideways through the middle to open it out, leaving a hinge;

put it between sheets of plastic wrap and flatten it with a meat hammer (the plastic minimises damage to the meat).

Melt the butter over a gentle heat. Season the meat quite highly with salt and pepper, and cover it with the rashers of bacon. Peel and stone the peach and the avocado and quarter them (don't let the avocado hang about unless you squeeze lemon juice over it to prevent it discolouring). Lay out the peach and avocado quarters along the bacon slices near one edge of the meat, dust them liberally with cornflour, and roll them up tightly in the beef. Cut a piece of kitchen foil big enough to wrap up the roll, with 10 to 13 cm (4 to 5 inches) extra at the sides. Brush the foil with melted butter and roll the beef up tightly in it, twisting the ends like a Christmas cracker to make the package airtight.

Cook for 40 minutes in the preheated oven, switch off and let the beef remain for a further 20 minutes. Unwrap the beef and cut thick slices with a sharp knife. Serve with a well-flavoured sauce, such as madeira sauce.

∼• ∼

The classic madeira sauce recommended by Ernst Stuhler is splendid, but a lot of work in a home kitchen not geared up for such things, since it involves several stages of concentrating good veal stock with flavourings, wine and thickenings. Unless you are feeling particularly energetic and ambitious, just make a good brown sauce or gravy that you are familiar with and flavour it with madeira or some other fortified wine such as port, marsala or sherry. An orange sauce of the type that often accompanies duck is also a possibility, or you could try replacing the orange with peaches, so long as it is not too sweet.

Hermann Schneider, whose restaurant is called Two Faces, turns one of them to the river and the other to the sea for a main dish of scallop mousse in trout – with truffles, if you happen to have an oak tree in your back garden, and a dog with a sensitive nose. Otherwise, you can leave them out.

# SCALLOP MOUSSE IN TROUT WITH WHITE WINE SAUCE

HERMANN SCHNEIDER, TWO FACES RESTAURANT, MELBOURNE

ENOUGH FOR 4 PEOPLE

| |
|---|
| **4 trout or small salmon trout, gutted** |
| **250 g (9 oz) scallops** |
| **2 egg whites** |
| **Salt and pepper** |
| **1 teaspoon lemon juice** |
| **Tabasco sauce to taste** |
| **250 ml (9 fl oz) double cream** |
| **40 g (1½ oz) butter** |
| **2 tablespoons flour** |
| *Garnish* |
| **Truffles** |
| *Stock* |
| **Fish trimmings** |
| **1 onion, 1 carrot, 1 leek, all roughly chopped** |
| **570 ml (1 pint) white wine** |

PREPARATION: Bone the trout without breaking the skin, putting them face down on a flat surface and pressing down hard on the backbone to loosen the bones. Turn the fish over and, with luck, you will be able to pull most of the bones out along with the backbone. Leave the head and tail on for the sake of appearance.

Make a fish stock. Take the fish trimmings and the chopped vegetables and simmer them for an hour in the white wine. Meanwhile, preheat the oven to 180°C (350°F, gas mark 4). Stand a bowl in ice. Purée the scallops in a blender, or push them through a mincer. Put the scallop purée in the chilled bowl, add the egg whites and beat until stiff. Fold in a little salt, pepper and lemon juice, and the tabasco sauce. Add 150 ml (¼ pint) cream bit by bit, stirring until the mousse is creamy and smooth. Spread mousse evenly over half the inside of each trout and fold them over back into their natural shape. Put them carefully into an oven dish. Strain the hot stock over the fish, cover the dish with kitchen foil and put it into the preheated oven for 8 to 10 minutes.

Take out the fish. Boil the stock hard on top of the stove while you gently skin the body of each trout, cutting the skin across at head and tail and down the back to make it easier to peel off.

Melt half the butter in a small saucepan, stir in the flour and cook for 2 to 3 minutes, but do not allow it to colour. Stir in the hot stock to make a smooth sauce. Over a low heat, stir in the rest of the cream and at the end the rest of the butter.

Serve the trout decorated with truffles, if used, and pour the sauce over.

# THE CLARE VALLEY, SOUTH AUSTRALIA

*'Sweet Auburn, loveliest village of the plain,*
*Where health and plenty cheer'd the labouring swain ...'*
Oliver Goldsmith, *The Deserted Village*

Many miles above the modestly charming city of Adelaide in South Australia is the Clare Valley, with a curling river that gives the lower part of the valley the name of Watervale, though what it is actually famous for is white wine.

It is no longer a particular advantage for a wine-maker to have big feet: otherwise, wine-making is one of the most unchanging of human activities. There are people who are pretentious, but wine itself is simple: it has a colour to look at, so you look at it; a smell to smell, so you smell it; a taste to taste, so you taste it. For the wine-makers there is also a harvest to celebrate, so they celebrate it, in Australia as in Europe (though some six months earlier than the European vintage, on account of the difference in hemisphere). Château Clare celebrates in a place with the same name as the deserted village in Goldsmith's poem. They set a whole day aside, and harvest lunch begins early, to allow plenty of time for eating and drinking.

Trestle tables with check cloths go up under an awning that looks like a pavilion at a medieval tournament, but it is hardly a dressy occasion – most people wear shorts or jeans. However, many a wine buff would gladly waive the formalities to be there when they broach last year's bottles for the first time. It is the tradition that the valley chefs compete to create a new dish for the celebration. The stew invented by Mark Fernandas of Brice Hill for the occasion is as Australian as any stew could be, but has a touch of international imagination as well.

Australian rabbits are the proud progeny of a dozen bunnies that came off the clipper *Lightning* in 1859 and bred and spread all over the country at a rate of something like eighty miles a year. There are not nearly as many as there used to be; but this is the effect of myxomatosis rather than rabbit stew. The one thing this stew doesn't have in it, oddly enough, is wine. Rabbit can be dry and stringy, so it's often marinated before cooking, though a youthful rabbit can be tender enough for quick frying. (One way of telling if your rabbit is a nice young rabbit is to look at its knees. Plump knees and flexible front legs are desirable – and not only in rabbits.)

Whatever you do with a rabbit, you start off doing it with onions – because rabbit and onions is one of the great love stories of the world. The use of prunes is characteristically Australian, but the nut, herb and garlic sauce is unusual – rather reminiscent of pesto, which the Italians put on their pasta, and which can also be used to enrich a meat dish.

# CLARE VALLEY RABBIT STEW, WITH PRUNES AND PEANUTS

MARK FERNANDAS, BRICE HILL VINEYARD RESTAURANT,
CLARE VALLEY

ENOUGH FOR 6 PEOPLE

| |
|---|
| **2 tender rabbits, jointed** |
| **2 to 4 onions, sliced** |
| **Olive oil for frying** |
| **1 bay leaf** |
| **4 ripe tomatoes, peeled and chopped** |
| **2 cloves of garlic, crushed in their skins** |
| **A handful of parsley** |
| **30 almonds, peeled and lightly toasted** |
| **125 ml (4 fl oz) water** |
| **Salt and pepper** |
| **75 g (3 oz) peanuts (can be salted)** |
| **20 prunes** |

PREPARATION: Fry one or two onions per bunny in olive oil over a medium heat until golden, then add a bay leaf and the chopped tomatoes – you can use tinned ones if you have to, though fresh, ripe ones are better. Toss the rabbit joints into this mixture, cover the pan and cook gently for half to three-quarters of an hour.

Pound the garlic, the parsley and the almonds in a mortar, then stir in the water – or whizz the lot in a blender. Add the blend to the stew. Season with salt and pepper. Continue cooking until the rabbit is tender, about another half-hour.

The peanuts and the prunes are hardly cooked at all – just simmered for 10 minutes in water, strained and added to the pot just before serving.

~ • ~

Clare's first winery still stands – a rather modest building resembling a Somerset cowshed – established by Jesuits for the official purpose of making sacramental wine. They produced a vintage which was even more full-bodied than sacramental wine is supposed to be; and their Seven Hill Winery became famous: vines are the first sight to greet the eyes of the parishioners every Sunday morning, as they leave their stumpy-towered stone church.

The pudding for the vintage lunch was cooked under the sign of the cross: with the presbytery cook, Susie Samuel, beating the egg-whites for a Pav below a large painted crucifix hanging on the kitchen wall. The Pav competes with steak for the honour of being the Australian national dish. If you want to be formal, call it Pavlova. It was invented in her honour when she came to dance in Australia. It is an outstandingly pretty dish, with a good combination of flavours, tastes and textures all in step with each other. It is fruit, cream and meringue – but not the simple sugar-and-egg meringue which you find in most British cookery books. The Pav is reliable, thanks to the addition of cornflour and a raising agent (cream of tartar) and to a quick blast of heat at the start of the baking process.

# PAVLOVA

### SUSIE SAMUEL, SEVEN HILL PRESBYTERY, CLARE VALLEY

### ENOUGH FOR 6 PEOPLE

| |
|---|
| **3 egg whites** |
| **$\frac{1}{2}$ teaspoon cream of tartar** |
| **175 g (6 oz) caster sugar and 2 teaspoons extra** |
| **$\frac{1}{2}$ tablespoon cornflour** |
| **1 teaspoon vanilla essence** |
| **1 teaspoon vinegar** |
| **225 g (8 oz) strawberries or other soft fruits** |
| **6 passion fruit** |
| **4 kiwi fruit** |
| **1 banana** |
| **Juice of $\frac{1}{2}$ lemon** |
| **275 ml ($\frac{1}{2}$ pint) double cream** |

PREPARATION: Preheat the over to 200°C (400°F, gas mark 6). Grease a baking sheet and line it with lightly greased greaseproof paper. Draw an 18 cm (7 inch) circle on the paper and sprinkle cornflour over the area. (This is a belt-and-braces job, because the Pav is too fragile to stand rough treatment to get if off if it sticks.)

Whisk the egg whites with the cream of tartar until they form soft peaks, then whisk in 175 g (6 oz) of caster sugar, a spoonful at a time. Mix in the cornflour, then carefully fold in ½ teaspoon vanilla essence and the vinegar. Spoon the meringue on to the paper circle, and shape it (usually as a cake or shell) with a knife. Put it into the middle of the oven and immediately turn the heat down to 100°C (200°F, gas mark ¼). The meringue should be dry in 1½ to 2 hours. While the meringue is baking, peel the fruit and cut it up elegantly. Squeeze the lemon juice over the banana to stop it discolouring. Whip the cream with the extra 2 teaspoons of caster sugar, adding the rest of the vanilla essence towards the end. The cream should be of an easy-spreading consistency. To minimise the risk of breakage, open the oven door and let the meringue cool before you take it out. Just before serving, cover the meringue all over, sides and top, with the cream, and decorate it with lots of fruit.

# TASMANIA

*'Come all ye gallant poachers, that ramble void of care,*
*That walk out on a moonlight night with dog and gun and snare:*
*The hare and lofty pheasant you have at your command,*
*Not thinking of your last career upon Van Diemen's Land.'*

So goes the British folksong, one of many lamenting the hardships of transportation. After Captain Cook had brought Australia to their attention (for other explorers had discovered it long before), it took the English Establishment only eight years to decide that the best use for a new-found land was to clear their gaols into it, thus founding a people with a deep-seated disrespect for class pretension and any kind of authority. (Since one of the evils of Britain is its class system, and one of the most dangerous things any nation can do is to believe its government, this was not by any means a bad thing.)

If the poachers were going today, they would be in their seventh heaven. Tasmania (which Tasman, who first took possession of it in the name of Holland, first called Van Diemen's Land after the Governor of the Dutch East Indies) lacks the harsh feel of much of the mainland landscape: it is like another British Isle; and if it feels slightly more exotic, that is often because it is less spoilt. It has winters, green meadows, apple orchards, mountains and forests. Here are two Esks where salmon run as they do in the North Yorkshire river and the Exe by Exeter, a Tamar, a Swansea, a Devonport, a Mersey, a Launceston (also a Rubicon, and several villages named after places in the *Arabian Nights* by the explorer Hugh Germain, who carried a copy as light relief from his other book, the Bible). There are stone bridges, churches, oak trees sprung of acorns from Windsor Great Park. There is even the odd old inn. And the game would not have displeased the English hunting squire of the early 1800s, nor the poacher sentenced to transportation by the squire, in his role of magistrate, on account of their mutual interest in duck, pheasant, hare, pigeon, salmon and deer.

Prospect House, Richmond, now a restaurant, is a genteel, white, early Victorian manor among lawns at the end of a drive. Inside, the antiques are younger than they would be in an English equivalent; but there is the same atmosphere of polished wood and log fires. They make a pigeon pie there that puffs out its pastry on top like the live bird being self-important with its chest. There are Tasmanian wines to drink, for though the wine industry there is very small and quite new it is already respected, making wines that have more of northern Europe in them than most Australian products.

Pigeon pie is what Squire Trelawney and the Doctor gave to young Jim Hawkins at the beginning of *Treasure Island*. This sort of romance is very difficult for a pigeon to live up to, and I am still waiting for one that does. The heartiness of the image seems particularly difficult to reconcile with the cautious chewing policy one has to adopt for fear of breaking the teeth on lead shot. But shooting is not a prerequisite. The dovecotes of country houses were not built only to encourage a bit of cooing in the park; and the birds that lived there were specially fed and fattened like other poultry. Look for youth and plumpness in a pigeon.

# PIGEON PIE

TOM SAMEK, PROSPECT HOUSE RESTAURANT, RICHMOND, TASMANIA

ENOUGH FOR AT LEAST 8 PEOPLE

| |
|---|
| 4 pigeons |
| Salt and pepper |
| 100 g (4 oz) speck (or *pancetta*, or fat green bacon), sliced |
| 2 teaspoons oil |
| 250 g (9 oz) lean beef, cut into strips |
| 250 g (9 oz) dried green peas, soaked overnight and drained |
| $\frac{1}{2}$ small head of celery, chopped |
| A bunch of spring onions, chopped |
| 1 bouquet garni |
| 3 eggs, hard-boiled and quartered |
| Thyme |
| A glass of port |
| 250 g (9 oz) pastry dough (Prospect House uses puff) |
| 125 ml (4 fl oz) soured cream |
| 2 pigeon livers |
| A little butter, melted |
| *Stock* |
| 4 pigeon carcasses |
| 2 onions, cut up in their skins |
| 1 or 2 leeks, chopped |
| 2 or 3 cloves of garlic, crushed |
| $\frac{1}{2}$ small head of celery, roughly chopped |
| 1 bouquet garni |
| Salt and pepper |
| 1 litre ($1\frac{3}{4}$ pints) water |
| 2 or 3 glasses of white wine |

PREPARATION: Cut the joints and meaty parts from the pigeons (keeping a look-out for lead shot if necessary).

Make the stock. Put the pigeon carcasses (hammered flat to encourage the flavour to come through) in a large saucepan with the stock vegetables, herbs and seasonings and the water and white wine. Bring to simmering point and simmer for 1 to 2 hours.

Season the pigeon segments. Chop half the speck into small pieces and fry gently, with a little oil to get it going, till the fat is coming out. Add the pigeon pieces and brown them. Layer the ingredients in a pie dish — beef, remaining speck, half the peas, the browned pigeon pieces, the celery and spring onions, and the bouquet garni. Make a final layer of the hard-boiled eggs and the rest of the peas. Sprinkle with thyme. Preheat the oven to 150°C (300°F, gas mark 2). Strain the stock. Heat the pan again with its juices and speck, and toss in a glass of port, followed by the stock. Leave it all to reduce while you roll out the pastry and cut it out to fit the top of the pie dish (you can take an impression of the outline by coating the rim of the dish with soured cream and laying the pastry on top). Cut a 2.5 cm (1 inch) strip all round the edge of the hole in the remaining pastry. Fix the strip around the edge of the pie dish, crimping it firmly over the edges.

When the sauce has reduced to rather less than the quantity needed, add the soured cream and shake the pan to mix it. Let it cook for a few moments, then add the pigeon livers and cook for another half minute. Strain the sauce into the pie and work the livers through the sieve on to the top.

Brush the pastry rim with more cream and cover the pie, sealing the edges carefully. Cut a cross in the top as a vent and brush with melted butter to glaze. Cook for 1½ hours.

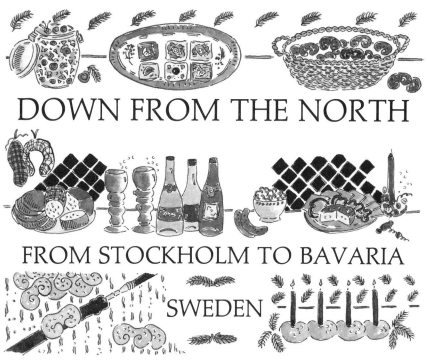

# DOWN FROM THE NORTH

## FROM STOCKHOLM TO BAVARIA

### SWEDEN

' "Cabbage revolts me."
"Why didn't you say so?"
"Because I loved you. I wanted to make a sacrifice for you." '
August Strindberg, *A Dream Play*

The Swedes are a well-organised people in a Protestant tradition: their recipes do not find it easy to be indulgent, but they have the virtue of being clear and practical – with none of the rambling Gothic of stage after stage of preparation which puts you off ever attempting many dishes from countries which are more distinguished gastronomically.

Sweden is a land of glorious summers as well as snowy winters, but its cooks did not start off with many of the advantages of the French or Italians – the tomatoes and peppers with the sun oozing out of them, other rich materials in plenty, wine and good society which are the encouragement of the southern cuisines. Sweden's prosperity – territorial before, consumerist today – is based on hard work, efficiency and natural resources; but the primeval Swedish cook trying to build up a national kitchen only occasionally had nature to help.

As soon as winter shut you in the house and gave you time to create, it took away your vegetables – even your eggs, for chickens lay less well in the dark days. The scattered rural society did not give you the everyday communal warmth which is the sauce to public cooking; nor an extensive aristocracy clamouring for treats. The preachies took away your enjoyment of alcohol and left you only drunkenness; the parson told you it was a sin to indulge yourself, anyway. There were — and are — compensations for the winter shortages (which before refrigeration and transport affected practically all communities to a greater or lesser degree): game, berries and mushrooms from the forest, fish from the sea, the streams and lakes; but monotony set in easily — disgruntled farm-hands would stipulate in their terms of engagement that salmon was not to appear on the table more than four or five times a week. Some parts of the country were so short of bread that they would spread their butter on dried fish.

Of course, it depended where you were: Skåne, in the far south, is the granary and orchard of Sweden: eating there was very different from eating in a forest cabin in the north. It also depended on the season — and the summer delights are far more of a joy when you are not able to have everything all the year round. As in Britain, recent years have brought tremendous improvements, as well as junk food; but Sweden's excellence remains in knowing how to handle its own raw materials properly, rather than in any repertoire of made-up dishes.

Though Swedish cooking tends to be simple and does not have a great range, there are some extremely good — and, for us who live further south, even exotic — things in it. There is not much point in giving an inhabitant of Chigwell a recipe for elk or reindeer; but these are an everyday option in the diet of a society whose mind is split between every sophistication the late twentieth century can offer, and the call of the wild.

What the Swedes love best about their country is their country. A camp fire (regulations permitting), a fresh-caught fish from the lake and a song by Evert Taube; and wilderness is Paradise Enow. There is an ingenious way of cooking a large fish on an open fire — wrap it in foil, then in layers of soaked newspapers. The wet newspapers moderate and spread the heat, so that the parcel can be put directly on the hot coals, and the foil seals in the flavours of the fish and the butter and herbs with which it is stuffed. A reasonably sized fish will be done by the time the coverings are charred.

The great Swedish treat is *gravlax* — marinated salmon — which is probably the least alarming raw fish dish in the world, as well as being one of the most distinguished. It can be made with other fish than salmon, mackerel among them (mackerel takes about half the time in the marinade), but seldom is, because the salmon is so good. (It is also quite an economical way of dealing

Australia: Avocado and Prawns in Ravigote Mayonnaise page 18

with an expensive fish, since most people eat less of something raw.)

*Grav* means 'buried', because once it would have been buried in the ground in a pot. Since the advent of refrigerators, you no longer need a spade – just a plastic bag. (Of course, the one thing the Swedes have not been terribly short of is refrigeration – we live with our deep-freezes, the Swedes live in theirs.) The quality of salmon is important in a dish which has virtually nothing else to it, not even cooking. Some farmed salmon is fatty, and people unused to it may find it too rich for them. The amount of sugar affects the consistency of the fish: the more sugar, the softer. It can be either a starter or main course (when it will be accompanied by its skin, fried, which is delicious, and boiled potatoes); but it is always served with a garnish of dill, and dill and mustard sauce. Other herbs can be used, but dill is the universal favourite, and rightly so. It ought to be as common as parsley in Britain, too.

# MARINATED SALMON
## (*Gravlax*)
### KIRSTIN HORNGREN, THE ISLAND OF TISTRONSKÄR,
### STOCKHOLM ARCHIPELAGO
### ENOUGH FOR 6 TO 8 PEOPLE

| |
|---|
| **1 kg (2¼ lb) middle cut of salmon or other firm fish, in two fillets** |
| **4 tablespoons salt** |
| **2 teaspoons white peppercorns, coarsely crushed** |
| **2 to 4 tablespoons sugar** |
| **A large bunch of fresh dill** |
| **You will also need a plastic bag** |

PREPARATION: Take out any remaining bones from the fillets, but do not skin them.

Mix the salt, pepper and sugar together in a bowl, and rub some of this mixture into the flesh of both fillets. Sandwich a thick pad of dill and plenty of seasoning mixture between the two fillets, skin side out (complementing the thinner section of one with the thicker part of the other). Put the salmon into the bag with plenty of dill and seasoning around it, press the air out of the bag and seal it. Marinate in the refrigerator for 2 days, turning once.

Drain the salmon and wipe or scrape off the spices. Slice it across, either with a thin slanting cut for hors-d'œuvre slices or, for a main course, in thick –

Sweden: Jansson's Temptation page 37

about 1 cm ($\frac{1}{2}$ inch) — slices, straight down. Skin before serving, and (if the pieces are not too small) fry the skin and serve it hot and crisp with the *gravlax*.

~ • ~

The quality of the mustard in the sauce is as exposed as the quality of the salmon. It should be the best plain mustard you can find. The Swedish taste is for sweet mustard. You may choose otherwise, and even reduce the amount of sugar in the recipe, though it needs some, but do not omit the dill if you can get hold of any.

# DILL AND MUSTARD SAUCE
### SWEDEN
### ENOUGH FOR 6 TO 8 PEOPLE

| |
|---|
| **3 tablespoons Dijon-type mustard** |
| **125 ml (4 fl oz) oil (not olive)** |
| **1 teaspoon salt** |
| **$\frac{1}{2}$ teaspoon white pepper** |
| **1$\frac{1}{2}$ tablespoons sugar** |
| **1 tablespoon red wine vinegar** |
| **Dill (or parsley or other herbs), finely chopped** |

PREPARATION: Use the same technique as for mayonnaise (though this is a less critical process). Put the mustard in the bowl and beat the oil into it: add the oil very slowly at first — it is not essential to do it drop by drop, as the books say, but whenever you see free oil in the bowl stop adding more and finish beating it in. When it is all in, add the other ingredients bit by bit, so that you can check the taste as you go. Add the dill last of all.

~ • ~

People also smoke their own fish a good deal in Sweden; and both *gravlax* and smoked salmon are common on the *smörgåsbord* — the Swedish institution which, the Swedes say, foreigners simply do not understand.

I do not find a buffet a perfect way of eating, and it is very easy to ruin the experience of a *smörgåsbord* for yourself through greediness. The spectacle of British or German tourists on a cruise ship let loose on a *smörgåsbord* is like a Roman orgy attended by Attila the Hun — the enjoyment is eclipsed by the confusion. The proper way to approach a *smörgåsbord* is with extreme restraint. A *smörgåsbord* is a four- or five-course meal which just happens to be all there at the same time: it is up to the diner to separate the courses and time them — salty fish, smoked fish, cold meats and salads, hot dishes, puddings. There is no hurry to pile a plate with any of them, not even the hot dishes: on a good *smörgåsbord* they are designed to hang around until the eaters catch up with them – and on a bad one they are unsatisfactory to begin with. Two long stayers are Jansson's Temptation and Swedish meatballs.

The Swedes eat so many meatballs that the insides of their stomachs must sometimes resemble a bowling alley. A standard recipe is two parts of ground beef to one each of veal and fat pork, mixed with finely chopped onion (fried), some crumbled rusk and a little milk. They are made rather small – sometimes hardly larger than new pennies – and are gently fried. The relish that usually accompanies them is a sweet preserve made from lingonberries, which are like small cranberries, and taste very similar.

Meatballs are everywhere in the world, but Jansson's Temptation is Sweden's own. Jansson was a legendary person who was tempted by the devil – and, we may assume, a comparatively easy tempt, since he did not rate dancing girls or anything really worth having, but a simple dish of potato, anchovy, onion and cream. However, this recipe for it comes from an elaborate setting: the Opera House Cellar, in Stockholm, a splendidly ornate building with a glittering clientele and plump chef, Werner Vögeli. The anchovies in the Temptation are not Mediterranean but Swedish anchovies – flavoured sprats which make the dish taste almost meaty rather than fishy. I rather prefer the Portuguese sort myself, but the taste is fiercer, so to emulate the Swedish they should be washed under the tap. A sweet onion is preferable to a ferocious one, and it is best to use old potatoes of a kind which don't go into a mush. The Temptation is ideal for parties (along with other temptations, for which I will not give the recipes just now).

# JANSSON'S TEMPTATION
## (*Jansson's Frestelse*)
### WERNER VÖGELI, OPERAKÄLLAREN, STOCKHOLM
### ENOUGH FOR 4 PEOPLE

| |
|---|
| 8 to 10 potatoes, cut into chips about 5 cm (2 inches) long and 5 mm ($\frac{1}{4}$ inch) thick |
| 1 Spanish onion, finely sliced |
| 20 anchovy fillets, rinsed, drained and cut into 1 cm ($\frac{1}{2}$ inch) lengths |
| 75 g (3 oz) butter |
| 275 ml ($\frac{1}{2}$ pint) single or double cream |
| 50 g (2 oz) toasted breadcrumbs |

PREPARATION: Preheat the oven to 200°C (400°F, gas mark 6). Butter a pie dish. Arrange a layer of potatoes on the bottom of the dish, then alternate layers of onions, anchovies, a few dabs of butter and potatoes, ending with a layer of potatoes. Pour the juice from the anchovy tins and half the cream over; and top with toasted breadcrumbs and more dabs of butter.

Cook for about 35 minutes, then pour the rest of the cream over the top and cook for a further 10 minutes.

*Smörgåsbord* is now everywhere in Swedish hotels and restaurants (it is exceedingly economical on staff); but it is in origin a festive board which has become commonplace in more prosperous times. The Swedish Christmas is even more of a festive season because of the prevailing darkness, and has kept much of its character as a fire festival – especially at Lucia, which ushers in the celebrations on 13 December.

Saint Lucia was a Christian martyr in Syracuse during the reign of Diocletian and – whatever the precise events of her martyrdom, whether or not they involved the apparition of burning fire around her temporarily invulnerable person – her name means 'light'. She is represented by hordes of little blonde girls with chaplets of candles on their heads and their stomachs stuffed with ginger biscuits and saffron buns – *Lussekatter*, Lucy Cats.

The shape of the 'cats' is pretty vague, but so is the central figure of the festival, who may just as well be that other light-bearer, Lucifer; and indeed the old name for these buns is *Doefvelskatter* – Devil's Cats. (In the forest lands in the north, Lusse was Lilith, queen of witches and fairies.) The buns are actually in the form of a characteristic Viking decoration – a ribbon with each end curled till it reaches the centre, one one way, one the other – but they have a raisin in the middle of the curl, which, to a child's imagination, does nicely for a moggy's eye.

# LUCY CATS
## (*Lussekatter*)
### MONIKA HÖRNER AND HER CHILDREN
### MAKES 24 CATS

| |
|---|
| About 1 teaspoon saffron filaments ($\frac{1}{4}$ teaspoon powder) |
| 1 tablespoon sugar |
| 1 teaspoon salt |
| 900 g (2 lb) strong white flour |
| 150 g (5 oz) butter |
| 50 g (2 oz) fresh yeast or 25 g (1 oz) dried yeast |
| 500 ml (17 fl oz) milk |
| 100 g (4 oz) raisins |
| 1 egg, beaten |

PREPARATION: Pound the saffron with some sugar. Stir the salt into the flour. Melt the butter in a saucepan, add the milk and warm it to about blood heat. Put the yeast in a bowl and pour the milk over it. Stir in the sugar/saffron mixture and the rest of the sugar. Stir until the sugar has dissolved. If you are using dried yeast, leave the mixture for a few minutes, until it froths. Stir in most of the flour and work it for a couple of minutes, until you have a soft dough that comes away from the sides of the bowl. Sprinkle with flour to prevent a crust forming, cover with a cloth and leave in a warm place for about 30 minutes, until its volume has doubled.

Grease 4 baking sheets. Take the dough out of the bowl and knead it well, for 5 minutes or more, on a flat surface, flouring it if necessary. Cut the dough into 4 pieces. Roll each quarter into a sausage on the board, and cut each sausage into 6 pieces. Roll each mini-sausage into a longer one, as thin as or thinner than your little finger. Form each ribbon into an S-shape, rolling each end of the strip back until it reaches the middle. Put it on to the baking sheet and decorate with a raisin in the centre of each roll. (Two S-shapes may be crossed over each other to make a double cat, which you will have to tell the children are Siamese *Lussekatter*.) Leave to rise in a warm place about as long as before. Preheat the oven to 230°C (450°F, gas mark 7).

Brush the cats with beaten egg to glaze them. Bake for 15–20 minutes.

While the children are eating cats, the festive treat for adults is *glögg*, red wine mulled with a good dash of spirits, sugar, orange peel, cinnamon and cardamom, and served with raisins and blanched almonds. (Most adult treats in Sweden tend to have alcohol in them; and the more of a treat they are, the less there is of anything else.)

After the holiday season comes the poverty and the clearing-up. This is a recipe for both – though *Pytt i Panna* is enough of an institution to be made in its own right. The idea of frying left-over meat with onions and potatoes is hardly earth-shattering, but do not scorn it: left-overs easily become horrors, and in this dish they are extremely tastily and prettily presented with the Bellman garnish, named after the Swedish eighteenth-century minstrel whose songs embody just that combination of good living and decorous lust that every Swede would like to emulate, if his grandfather's parson would let him.

# SWEDISH HASH À LA BELLMAN
## (*Pytt i Panna*)
### HANNES AND KALLE, TWO JOLLY BACHELORS, STOCKHOLM
### ENOUGH FOR 4 PEOPLE

| |
|---|
| Oil (not olive) or oil and butter for frying |
| Salt and pepper |
| 8 to 10 medium potatoes, diced |
| 2 or 3 Spanish onions, finely chopped |
| About 450 g (1 lb) cooked lean lamb or beef, diced |
| 200 g (7 oz) ham, diced |
| *Garnish* |
| 4 egg yolks |
| Pickled beetroot |
| Pickled cucumber |

PREPARATION: In separate pans (or one after the other), fry (and season): the potatoes on a fairly high heat until browning but not quite cooked; the onions on medium heat until soft; the lamb or beef on medium heat for a few minutes. Toss in the ham with the meat and cook a minute or two more. Then put everything together and carry on frying until the potatoes are completely cooked and everything is heated through.

Put a raw egg yolk in the centre of each plate and arrange concentric circles of pickled beetroot and cucumber around it. Surround it with hash.

Either I am chauvinist about it, or the common-or-garden apple is surprisingly fastidious about its geography. Put it in the South of France and it turns into that simpering creature, the Golden Delicious; in Scandinavia it becomes a sober-sided Gravenstein or one of a variety of rather small, sourish objects which make me long for that glory of Creation, a Cox's Orange Pippin.

But if there is one thing that northern Europe can make, it is a good apple cake. This one can be eaten hot or cold, but in either case is complemented by a cold vanilla custard.

# SWEDISH APPLE CAKE
## HANNES, OLJELUND, STOCKHOLM
### ENOUGH FOR 4 PEOPLE

| |
|---|
| About 100 g (4 oz) pounded rusks or fine breadcrumbs |
| 3 tablespoons butter |
| 6 apples, peeled and sliced |
| 4 tablespoons water |
| 100 g (4 oz) sugar |

PREPARATION: Preheat the oven to 200°C (400°F, gas mark 6). Butter a pie dish. If you are using breadcrumbs, fry them in butter until they are golden. Put the apple slices in the pie dish with a splash of water and strew the sugar over them. Dredge them with the rusks or breadcrumbs. Or, if you like, layer the apples and the rusks. Top with dabs of butter.

Bake for about 30 minutes, or until the top is a rich golden brown.

# VANILLA SAUCE
## HANNES, OLJELUND, STOCKHOLM
### ENOUGH FOR 4 PEOPLE

| |
|---|
| 2 egg yolks |
| 1 tablespoon sugar |
| 2 teaspoons cornflour |
| 425 ml ($\frac{3}{4}$ pint) milk |
| $\frac{1}{2}$ a vanilla pod or a few drops of vanilla essence |
| 125 ml (4 fl oz) double cream |

PREPARATION: Put the egg yolks into a saucepan with the sugar, cornflour and vanilla. Beat, then add milk over a low heat until the mixture thickens, being careful not to let it boil. Pour it into a serving dish and stir it occasionally until it is cool. Before serving, whip the cream stiff and fold it into the sauce.

*'The night is full of cooks ... the moon a little potato, every star a dumpling.'* Günter Grass,
*The Wicked Cooks*

The West Germans are mighty consumers of everything, from beer to
Beethoven: and their country is crammed not only with the possessions they
have earned in the rebuilt Germany but with the bygones of a busy past.

Germany has not much in the way of a middle − and not only because its
former capital is now an urban island in East Germany. It has always been an
assembly job of tribes, principalities or federal regions. The lumping-together
of Hitler's Germany has not removed the distinctions of geography, history,
religion. The thirteen million East Germans who settled in the West after the
war have settled, but not swamped: the two million Turkish 'guest' workers
are still guests. The supermarket has broadened but not abolished regional
tastes in food; and they are apt to come to the surface at times of celebration.

# SCHLESWIG-HOLSTEIN

*... that is the question.'* Hamlet

Germany and Denmark wrangled for thirteen columns of my *Encyclopaedia
Britannica* over the bottom chunk of the Jutland peninsula; and if, after a
thousand years, Germany has ended up with the land, things Nordic remain.

The way people drink is the way of the north − strong drink, often in gulps,
to put the sun in the belly when it does not shine in the sky. They like schnapps
chilled to a near-icicle, with a crudely named nibble on the top of the glass:
gull-dropping, they call it − a slice of liver sausage topped with a little puddle
of German mustard. Hardly persuades you to try it, somehow. Grog is the
quaff of the coast: rum with hot water and a lump of sugar, the sort of drink
you read about in Dickens. And they are arch, as if they were half-guilty about
it, in the manner of the would-be-would-be-not teetotal Protestant north. After
dinner they drink Pharisees − rum, coffee, whipped cream − so called because
the parson found his was the only cup without, and in his anguish (at the
wickedness of his flock) so accused them.

As if Schleswig-Holstein was not already sufficiently confused about its
nationality, it has chosen to make Camembert one of its products, along with
its own pale yellow Marsh Cheese, beech-smoked hams, and smoked eel

*Mettwurst*, a well-flavoured sausage traditionally hung in the smoke-houses in which they cure eels like the Dutch, Baltic salmon like the Swedes, and make *Schillerlocken*, strips of fish rolled into spirals round sticks.

Apart from having water-meadows that look like Holland and sandy, windy coasts that look like Denmark, Schleswig-Holstein has what it likes to call its Switzerland, in which perceptive foreigners are able to detect mild undulations almost without difficulty. Here, the Kletkamp estate (with a lot of old brick and Dutch gables) has been owned for ten generations by the Counts of Brokdorff, a family who have come to keeping their white mansion alive by marketing stately ambience to humbler folk, such as a local farmer celebrating his fiftieth birthday. His menu was thoroughly local – and in this land of pastures between two seas that is no restriction at all. The main course was fried steak with a prune and rum sauce, steak *à la* Husum; which was preceded by shrimp soup *à la* Busum. Husum and Busum are local towns, and if the menu was longer, there would be no problem adding to it with food named after Bargum, Breklum, Struckum, Stadum, Risum, Karlum, Böglum and Bordelum.

The chef, Holger Urmersbach, came from a nearby restaurant of some reputation. He is one of those chef-patrons who are so professional and undemonstrative that the dish seems to assemble itself from some invisible kitchen under the table; but with Busum Shrimp Soup he did have the advantage of a ready-made crab soup concentrate that in Germany can be bought in chunks, like orange cheese, and melted down. In Britain, you would have to substitute a good tin – or, of course, your own makings. To go between the schnapps on the lawns to start and the Pharisees on the lawns to finish, the lunch in the tall blue and white dining room included plenty of rum in the sauce for the steak and plenty of brandy in the soup.

# BUSUM SHRIMP SOUP
## HOLGER URMERSBACH, KLETKAMP ESTATE, SCHLESWIG-HOLSTEIN
### ENOUGH FOR 4 PEOPLE

| |
|---|
| 300 g (11 oz) shrimps in their shells |
| 1 large onion, finely diced |
| 25 g (1 oz) butter |
| 275 ml ($\frac{1}{2}$ pint) white wine |
| 2 tablespoons brandy |
| About 700 ml ($1\frac{1}{4}$ pints) hot water or crab soup |
| Salt and pepper |
| Sugar to taste |
| 50 g (2 oz) crab soup concentrate (unless using made soup) |
| 2 egg yolks |
| *Garnish* |
| 250 ml (9 fl oz) *crème fraîche* or soured cream |
| Chives, chopped |

PREPARATION: Peel the shrimps, but keep the shells. Soften the onion in butter, then add the shrimp shells, wine and splash of brandy. When the mixture comes to the boil, add the water, season roughly with salt, pepper and sugar (careful!) and boil for 15 minutes. Melt the crab soup concentrate in a saucepan, add the rest of the brandy, strain in the stock and boil for 10 minutes more. Correct the seasoning (and the strength, if necessary).

Keep a little soured cream back for decoration, and beat the egg yolks with the rest of the cream in a bowl to make a liaison. Add the shrimps to the soup, take it off the heat and stir in the liaison. Pour the soup into warmed bowls and decorate with chopped chives and a blob of soured cream.

*Rote Grütze* is the summer pudding of the North – fruit with a thickening of cornflour, served cold or hot with vanilla cream. (Cold every time, for me.) It is sometimes called Blushing Girl – presumably because it's red, and wobbles interestingly. You may call it Blushing Person if you prefer.

Since there had been so much alcohol in the previous two courses, they only put burgundy in the pud – and nothing at all in the vanilla cream. This is a marvellous pudding, as it ought to be, given the ingredients.

# BLUSHING GIRL
## (*Rote Grütze*)
THE COUNTESS OF BROKDORFF, KLETKAMP ESTATE,
SCHLESWIG-HOLSTEIN

ENOUGH FOR 4 PEOPLE

| |
|---|
| **250 ml (9 fl oz) redcurrant juice** |
| **250 g (9 oz) sugar** |
| **A glass of burgundy or other red wine** |
| **2 tablespoons cornflour** |
| **200 g (7 oz) each of strawberries, raspberries, Morello cherries and redcurrants** |

PREPARATION: Heat the redcurrant juice and add the sugar and the wine. Smooth the cornflour with a little water and use it to thicken the juice.

Boil the mixture for a few minutes. Add the fruits, mixing them well in but being careful not to break them. When they are mixed, take the pudding off the heat, pour it into the serving bowl (or a mould – it should just hold a shape). Chill before serving.

# VANILLA CREAM
HOLGER URMERSBACH, KLETKAMP ESTATE, SCHLESWIG-HOLSTEIN

ENOUGH FOR 4 PEOPLE

| |
|---|
| **2 egg yolks** |
| **2 tablespoons sugar** |
| **1 vanilla pod** |
| **150 ml ($\frac{1}{4}$ pint) double or single cream** |

PREPARATION: Beat the egg yolks and sugar together. Slit the vanilla pod with a sharp knife, scrape out the inside of one or both halves of the pod and add to the bowl. Continue beating while you add the cream.

# THE RHINELAND PALATINATE

*In which the way to the Hardt is through the stomach.*

The Pfalz, the Rhineland Palatinate, and Alsace are near neighbours. Alsace was much fought over, and is now French. The Palatinate was also fought over, and is now German. When the country is not being fought over, it smiles – with sunshine enough to grow figs, peaches, lemons and tobacco; but above all, vines. The wine road runs north from the French border along the foothills of the Hardt mountains, and in due course passes the best of the Palatinate estates. Among the vines are picturesque villages with black and white half-timbering made exotic by creepers and flowers.

At the time of the vintage the people of the Rhineland Palatinate celebrate by drinking new wine from last year's crop and eating onion tart. One particular onion tart was made by the lady of the Battenberg estate, which once belonged to one of our own most noble families, before they renounced German citizenship over half a century ago, and called themselves Mountbatten. Her kitchen was in a long white house forming one side of a courtyard of old barns, with a dog and a tractor sleeping on the warm stones. With its hearty flavours, *Zwiebelkuchen* is a good dish for real men who don't eat quiche; and to make it even more like a pizza than a tart, you can toughen the dough by using strong flour and less yeast, and letting it rise for longer.

# ONION TART
## (*Zwiebelkuchen*)

THE LADY OF THE BATTENBERG ESTATE, RHINELAND PALATINATE

ENOUGH FOR 4–6 PEOPLE

| |
|---|
| **125 ml (4 fl oz) warm milk** |
| **50 g (2 oz) butter** |
| **20 g ($\frac{3}{4}$ oz) fresh yeast or 2 teaspoons dried yeast** |
| **$\frac{1}{2}$ teaspoon salt** |
| **250 g (9 oz) flour** |
| **200 g (7 oz) smoked bacon, cut into strips** |
| **1 tablespoon lard** |
| **1 kg ($2\frac{1}{4}$ lb) onions, diced** |
| **$\frac{1}{2}$ teaspoon cumin seeds** |
| **Pepper** |
| **125 ml (4 fl oz) cream** |
| **2 egg yolks** |

PREPARATION: Warm the milk just enough to melt the butter and crumble in fresh yeast or sprinkle in dried. If you are using dried yeast, leave the mixture in a warm place for 10 minutes or so, until it is frothy. Add half the salt to the flour and mix in the liquid. Knead, and leave to rise for 20 minutes in the warm. Grease a baking tray. Roll out the dough and place it on the baking tray, raising a small rim to stop the onions from escaping. Leave to rise again for 20 minutes. Preheat the oven to 200°C (400°F, gas mark 6).

Fry the bacon lightly in the lard, then add the onions, cover the pan and continue to cook until the onions soften. Season with cumin, pepper and the rest of the salt. Take the onion and bacon mixture off the heat and stir in the cream and the egg yolks. Spread the filling on the tart and bake for 30 minutes.

❧

They quaff wine rather than sip it in the Palatinate; for they have a lot of wine which is the sort you drink and enjoy, rather than drink and remember. They love festivities, the biggest and noisiest of which is the Sausage Fair at Bad Dürkheim, which does for the grape what Munich does for the hop. There are celebrations of the rose and the radish; Deidesheim Billy Goat Auction on Whit Tuesday; the Frogs' Leg Feast of Lachen-Speyerdorf in April; Gimmeldingen with its Almond Blossom Festival; and Blessing the Chestnuts at Edenkoben, where Ludwig I of Bavaria built his summer palace, Ludwigshöhe, below one of the many hill-top castles.

And whenever they have a festivity out come the stomachs. Every dish needs the participation of one stomach: but the *Pfälzer Saumagen* requires two, to make a treat so rustic that if the EEC had ever been told about it officially, they would probably have offered it a subsidy under the Common Agricultural Policy.

The second stomach belongs to a sow. *Pfälzer Saumagen* is like a haggis, only with more up-market meat; or like an over-organic Cornish Pasty, since it also contains diced potato; or like a sausage, only bigger, and with three holes instead of two. This is typical of stomachs, you understand – but it means you have to tie up two of them before you start. Leave the rest of the preparation to the professionals. Whatever you do, you do not want to confront the untreated object, even to blow up and play football with. Should you ever get hold of such a thing, you will find that it looks as if they *have* been playing football with it, on the slaughterhouse floor, with extra time. Even empty, it smells. It has floppy bits hanging off, and you don't know what to do with them. Cleaning a stomach at home is real fun, involving a lot of washing, trimming, a bit of light scraping, a good soak in salted water and blanching. Fortunately, the only people who are likely to have to do it are those who kill their own pigs, and they will probably be used to such things.

Being of no value, a pig's stomach goes straight into the waste pot at the slaughterhouse. There should be no difficulty in diverting one to the cleaning room, where it will be emptied, hosed in and out and put in an umbrella tripe machine, which works rather like an automatic dishwasher, except that it abrades slightly as well, before being blanched. If you have a small independent butcher who deals personally with the slaughterhouse, all you have to do is to deal personally with him, and get him to order one. If your butcher is part of a chain, he is not likely to have any direct contact, and getting anything unusual like stomach or ears will be impossible, too much trouble, or dependent on whatever system the chain has to handle such queries.

# STUFFED STOMACH OF SOW
## (Pfälzer Saumagen)
THE LÀDY OF THE BATTENBERG ESTATE, RHINELAND PALATINATE
STOMACH TO STOMACH RATIO = 1 SOW TO 10 ADVENTUROUS PEOPLE

| |
|---|
| **A cleaned pig's stomach** |
| **2 large potatoes, diced** |
| **2 litres (3½ pints) stock or water** |
| **2 large onions, finely chopped** |
| **Lard for frying** |
| **700 g (1½ lb) lean pork, diced** |
| **700 g (1½ lb) sausage meat** |
| **3 eggs** |
| **A good handful of parsley, finely chopped** |
| **2 heaped teaspoons each of chopped marjoram, ground coriander and paprika** |
| **1 tablespoon salt** |
| **Plenty of pepper** |
| **And you'll need some string** |

PREPARATION: Conquer your aversion to the stomach, and tie up 2 of the 3 apertures.

Parboil the diced potato in the stock (about 5 minutes), while softening the chopped onions in lard. In a bowl, mix well the diced pork, sausage meat, onions, potato cubes, eggs and seasonings (in plenty).

Stuff the stomach cheerfully, with some care to avoid weakening it, tying up any holes you make in it by accident. Tie up the remaining opening, excluding air and pressing the stuffing solid, but leaving a little space for expansion.

Put the stomach in the hot stock and simmer it for 3 hours. Leave it to cool in the stock. You can use the stock for soup afterwards (if it is well flavoured, keep a cup for the next recipe). Cut into quite thick slices – about 1 cm ($\frac{1}{2}$ inch) – and fry them in lard.

This dish is particularly good for sending shivers down the spines of unsuspecting guests you never want to see again. However, it is only the idea of the stomach that is off-putting and, when they come to think about it, most people will realise that they have eaten thousands of far worse guts encasing sausages. Tripe and haggis eaters will have no problem at all – and this filling is made of tastier and far higher-quality material than haggis. You might even get the kids to eat it, if you told them it was a hamburger.

Should you come across a bottle, you might accompany this dish with the wine named after it – Kallstadter Saumagen. In any case, sauerkraut on one side of the plate will contrast with the rich meaty flavour of sliced and fried *Saumagen* on the other.

Sauerkraut is a well-travelled dish: the recipe may have come from China. It is usually bought ready made, but is not at all difficult to make, provided that you do not object to the smell of fermenting cabbage. The cabbage is sliced very thinly, and layered in a bowl, each layer being sprinkled with salt – and perhaps some juniper berries. The cabbage is then kept pressed down for 3 to 6 weeks. When it has stopped fermenting, replace the brine with fresh water and take it out as you need it.

There are lovers of unadorned sauerkraut, but having gone through the mental turmoil of the relationship with your stomach, you might as well continue to go the whole hog. This recipe can be used with ordinary cabbage as well.

# SAUERKRAUT
## THE LADY OF THE BATTENBERG ESTATE, RHINELAND PALATINATE
### ENOUGH FOR 8 TO 10 PEOPLE

| |
|---|
| 2 onions, chopped |
| 1 tablespoon lard |
| 1 kg (2¼ lb) sauerkraut |
| 275 ml (½ pint) good stock |
| 1 glass Riesling |
| 1 tablespoon vinegar |
| About 1 teaspoon each salt and sugar |
| 2 bay leaves |
| 1 teaspoon cumin seeds |
| 4 juniper berries |
| 2 cooking apples, peeled, cored and diced |

PREPARATION: Fry the onions in the lard till they are golden. Add the sauerkraut, stock, Riesling, vinegar, salt, sugar, bay leaves and spices, and mix together. Put the apples on top of the sauerkraut mixture. Cover the pan and cook gently for as little as 15 minutes (to my taste) or 45 minutes or more for a dish which is more homogenous.

# BAVARIA

*'Only a dunderhead digs a knife in his dumpling ...'* Bavarian saying

Southern Germany stretches between France and Austria via the Black Forest, Swabia and Bavaria; and the influences of both countries are felt in its cooking, among other things. These Germans tend to be Catholics rather than Protestants; they prefer indulgence to abstinence, and elaboration to plainness.

This is dumpling country, the most delicate being the Swabian, which are a kind of informal noodle; but most try to take life lightly. *Semmelknödeln* are bread dumplings with onion and parsley, rather like an exterior stuffing, and very tasty. They should be as light as possible, which means not manhandling them when forming them into balls. The best of their kind are so gently put together that they break apart in their cooking water if it boils, though they have become stronger than that by the time they have risen to the top to show that they are done. What you are trying to create is a dumpling as light as a cloud on a summer's day.

Germany: Busum Shrimp Soup page 44

# SAVOURY DUMPLINGS
## (*Semmelknödeln*)
### THE LANDLORD OF THE STADT MÜNCHEN, LANDSBERG, BAVARIA
### ENOUGH FOR 4 PEOPLE

| |
|---|
| 250 ml (9 fl oz) milk |
| 8 white bread rolls or slices of bread, a day old, broken into small pieces |
| 1 onion, finely chopped |
| 1 tablespoon butter or dripping |
| 3 eggs |
| A bunch of parsley, finely chopped |
| Salt and white pepper |

PREPARATION: Bring the milk to the boil and pour it over the pieces of bread. Cover, and leave until the bread is soft. Soften the onion in the butter in a covered pan set over a low heat. Bring a good-sized saucepan of water to the boil. Break the eggs on to the bread, add the parsley and season well with salt and pepper. Mix just enough, but don't mangle, tossing up the dough with the fingertips rather than squeezing it, only patting it together gently at the end. With wet hands, roll the mixture into dumplings about 5 cm (2 inches) across. Put them carefully into the hot water and simmer for about 20 minutes.

Bavarians love dumplings – and they love beer. With thousands of different brews all over the country, it takes quite a lot of devotion for a German to do his – or her – patriotic duty by the national drink. Fortunately, the Germans are exceedingly patriotic in this respect, none more so than the Bavarians – and not only at the time of the Munich *Oktoberfest*.

Aided and abetted by substantial waitresses with arms like piano-heavers, Munich drinkers support the principle that it is an excellent thing to eat between meals, and especially honour the ritual of the sausage and the ritual of the *Radi*.

The *Radi* is not a little British white-bottomed-blushing-topped radish. It is a dragon among radishes, deathly pale and big enough to hit people with. The Bavarians slice it very thinly with their personal radish-knife (which they carry around with them because they say the ones from the beer-garden are never sharp enough), sprinkle salt between the slices to extract the juices, and

France: Pear Charlotte page 72

eat it with pretzels or bread and butter. A slicer of greater bravado may cut it in a spiral, as if peeling an apple. It is quite delicious, and less fattening than peanuts, but nothing to the *Weisswurst*.

Served afloat in little bowls of hot water, *Weisswurst* are dipped into the local sweet mustard and sucked out of their pallid skins in a suggestive manner. They do not travel well. In fact, they do not travel at all. Like bread, *Weisswurst* were traditionally made early in the morning (mainly from such things as veal, calves' brains and parsley); and even in Munich, it is said that no *Weisswurst* should be suffered to survive the stroke of noon. The Bavarians – a lively, pleasure-loving people who have forgotten neither their cultural heritage nor their political past as an important and successful kingdom – call this sausage 'Lucullus's index finger' and a 'Bavarian banana', and speak of 'the *Weisswurst* equator': north of which, eventually, are the Prussians (which, to a Bavarian and a southerner, cannot be considered wholly a good thing). On a good day in the October beer festival, getting on for half a million *Weisswurst* may be eaten, to quote only one of the bulging statistics of indulgence from this extraordinary event. Naturally, a hard life of eating and drinking takes its toll. Sometimes the Munichunians need a break: in which case they visit a country hostelry and drink there instead, helped by a lunch of dumplings, veal and mushroom soup.

# MUSHROOM SOUP
## (*Schwammerlsuppe*)
### THE LANDLORD OF THE STADT MÜNCHEN, LANDSBERG, BAVARIA
#### ENOUGH FOR 4 PEOPLE

| |
|---|
| 1 litre (1¾ pints) beef stock |
| 250 g (9 oz) mushrooms, thinly sliced |
| 1 onion, finely chopped |
| 1 tablespoon butter |
| Salt and white pepper |
| 2 tablespoons flour |
| 125 ml (4 fl oz) cream |
| A handful of parsley, chopped |
| 2 egg yolks, beaten |

PREPARATION: Heat the stock. Begin to soften the onion in the butter, adding the mushrooms almost immediately. Season with salt and pepper, stir in the flour, add the hot stock and simmer for 15 minutes. Make a liaison by mixing the cream and the parsley with the egg yolks, and just before serving take the soup off the heat and beat the liaison in.

The principle of cooking *Kalbshaxe* (knuckle of veal) is to boil it and braise it, which both tenderises and glazes a coarse cut which often finds a humbler destiny. The boiling (which can be done in advance) makes a stock which is then concentrated and used for the basting.

# KNUCKLE OF VEAL
## (*Kalbshaxe*)
THE LANDLORD OF THE STADT MÜNCHEN, LANDSBERG, BAVARIA

ENOUGH FOR 4 PEOPLE

| |
|---|
| **1 knuckle of veal with plenty of meat on it (about 1 kg/2¼ lb)** |
| **200 g (7 oz) veal bones, preferably the gelatinous bones from the breast, chopped** |
| **2 onions, halved** |
| **2 leeks, halved** |
| **2 cloves** |
| **2 bay leaves** |
| **10 peppercorns** |
| **Salt** |
| **Stock or water to cover** |
| **1 carrot, halved** |
| **1 stick of celery, chopped** |
| **1 tablespoon dripping** |

PREPARATION: Put the meat, bones, onions, leeks and seasonings in a large pan and pour in stock or water to cover. Bring to the boil and simmer, uncovered, till the meat is tender (about 1 hour). About 10 minutes before the end, concentrate some stronger veal stock by frying the carrot and celery in dripping in a roasting tin, adding about 750 ml (1¼ pints) of stock and boiling it down by two-thirds. Preheat the oven to 200°C (400°F, gas mark 6).

Put the meat into the roasting tin, and leave the remaining broth boiling. Brown the meat in the hot oven for 20 to 30 minutes, basting frequently with the stock in the tin, and adding more broth as that dries up.

Serve with the vegetables and gravy from the tin, and *Semmelknödeln*.

# TO COUNTRIES OF THE SUN

# FRANCE, ITALY AND PORTUGAL

# FRANCE

*'The more you cook, the more you love it. It's like a painter – one day spectacular, the other not. Imagination is very important in the kitchen. Anybody can cook with experience: but when you love your business in your heart, you are an artist.'* M. Delfer, chef-proprietor of L'Auberge de la Belle Aventure in the Forest of Rambouillet

The question no Briton can escape as he stands on the White Cliffs of Dover is 'Why do the lot over there have food like that, and we have food like this?' There is no single explanation, but there is a simple answer. The reason is – everything.

The French know what they are doing when it comes to food. They do not muddle through. The national inclination towards being both analytical and practical is just the thing for the kitchen: they have tended to develop systems of cookery through the ideas not only of great chefs but also of philosophers of the kitchen like Brillat-Savarin; and whereas individuals and individual recipes move around at random and get lost easily, systems marshal people's abilities, and build on them.

The French have never lost their contact with their land – and they approach it not over a carpet of daffodils but through the stomach. *Déjeuner sur l'herbe* requires, first and foremost, *déjeuner.* Not only are they maniacal hunters and fishermen, secure in the personal conviction that, if the hydraulics in the Citroën should ever spring a leak far from home, they can live off the land till they get to the next café; but they have not become detached from the countryside. Their industrial revolution came much later than the British, and even the city-dweller is likely to have relatives – or, at the least, recent forefathers – in the country.

Nor was the French peasant as efficiently dispossessed of land ownership as the British agricultural labourer: he had a stake in what he produced, as well as a grower's knowledge of it. This has made markets better – and helped them to survive. The monoliths of mass food manufacture and distribution are only pebbles by comparison with the British, and far less boring.

Some countries have either good cooking for aristocrats or good cooking by peasants, but France has both, and a splendid bourgeois tradition as well as high-quality professionals. It all works together: people without any natural talent for cooking absorb a minimum level of skill because it is expected of them; amateur cooks behave like professionals; chefs have dignity and are well trained. France has her convenience foods, but they are more than packaged convenience. The salads and meats of the *traiteur*, the pâtés and sausages of the *charcutier* are often made to a standard which most home cooks cannot surpass. They lead, rather than downgrade.

Restaurants are well patronised and valued – a compliment which most restaurants return by working hard and not rooking the public. Alongside the smallholders and the small tradespeople are the *chefs-propriétaires* and restaurant families whose work is, if not all their life, at least a great deal of it.

Even the faults of the French (of which the British are extremely conscious) contribute to the quality of their food. They are liable to conceit and chauvinism, so they exalt their local products, which improve as a result (when British specialities expire in a bog of indifference). Being by nature highly territorial, they lay down the law, argue and complain. How wonderfully they complain – and how valuable are their complaints. There is no single factor that has contributed more to the poverty and expense of British public food than that pathetic response to the waiter's question – 'Very nice, thank you.'

The geography of France provides ingredients from the sun, from the rain; from the Atlantic, from the Mediterranean; from the mountains, the lowlands, the garden, the vineyard. (The last is important: wine makes for creative cooking, as it seems to make for lively people.) And being both a colonial and a continental power, France has been well placed to absorb new foods and influences from abroad.

But the simple answer to the Briton on the White Cliffs of Dover is: they care. By no means all the food in France is good food, but the topic is a near-universal passion: announce that you are just about to put a light under a *pot-au-feu*, and scarcely a nostril in the nation will fail to twitch.

# LORRAINE

*'It is not forever, 1873'*
*'It was not forever, 1920'*
*'Forever united, 1946'*
Inscription at Notre Dame de Sion, La Colline Inspirée

Lorraine, whose twin cross became the symbol of de Gaulle's Free French, was, like Alsace on the other side of the Vosges mountains, German for half a century after the Franco-Prussian War. But where other provinces speak their own identities before they speak their country's, Lorraine says 'France' before it says 'Lorraine'.

It rolls or it is flat, it is cabbages or cows, pasture or vine, orchard or woodland – but it is always green, usually broad, and often wet. A pattern of furrows, great and small – little furrows of ploughs, broad furrows of rivers – the Marne, the Meuse, the Moselle. There is industry too – old heavy industry north of Metz (traditionally the commercial centre), newer industry in the south, in and around Nancy, where the Dukes of Lorraine had their capital.

In Nancy, in a house that once belonged to General Count Léopold Hugo, father of Victor Hugo, is La Gentilhommière restaurant. The Count would probably not have approved of the pink neon name arching over the door, but the kitchens might well have appealed to his military mind, with rows of lustrous copper pans neatly ranged in order of size, as if it were only a matter of time before the smallest omelette pan grew up to be a stockpot.

The specialities of the house include Saddle of Lamb with Mushrooms in Season – and the more interesting the variety of mushroom, the more interesting the dish. There are two parts to it – the lamb and a mould of the other ingredients. Though showy, the mould is not at all difficult, especially if you have a food processor. The lamb is even easier: only the lean eye of the meat is used, with all bone and fat trimmed away, but this is boning of the simplest, and your butcher will do it for you with pleasure, the saddle not being the cheapest of cuts. (A saddle is a double loin, and may be cut short or long; one side only may be enough for four.)

# SADDLE OF LAMB WITH MUSHROOMS IN SEASON

LA GENTILHOMMIÈRE RESTAURANT, NANCY, LORRAINE

ENOUGH FOR 4 PEOPLE WITH REFINED APPETITES

| |
|---|
| **Pretty vegetables to line the mould (optional)** |
| **100 g (4 oz) shallots, finely chopped** |
| **50 g (2 oz) butter** |
| **200 g (7 oz) fresh mushrooms, chopped** |
| **2 egg whites** |
| **100 g (4 oz) chicken breast** |
| **200 ml (7 fl oz) *crème fraîche* or double cream** |
| **A glass of port** |
| **Salt and pepper** |
| **About 700 g (1½ lb) loin of lamb (trimmed and boned weight)** |
| **Thyme** |
| **Oil for frying** |

PREPARATION: Preheat the oven to 180°C (350°F, gas mark 4). Butter 2 ramekins well and, if you like, put in the bottom (soon to be the top) a decoration such as a cross of 2 cooked French beans with thin slices of cooked carrot in the quarterings.

Fry the shallots in a little butter until they are golden, then mix in about a third of the mushrooms (which should be lightly cooked and lose some of their liquid). Put the contents of the pan into a processor and add the egg whites, the chicken breast and 2 tablespoons of the cream. Blend. Put the paste into the ramekins on top of the decoration. Pour hot water into a bain-marie or roasting dish and put in the ramekins. Cook for 15 minutes in the preheated oven.

Fry the remaining shallot in butter, adding the rest of the mushrooms and, shortly afterwards, a glass of port, the rest of the cream and salt and pepper to taste. Leave this reducing while you powder the lamb with salt and sprinkle a broad stripe of thyme on either side, pressing the thyme well into the meat. Brown the lamb on both sides in oil and then cook it in the oven for 10 minutes. Slice the meat and turn out the ramekins. Arrange elegantly with the mushroom sauce poured around.

Lorraine wines are light: rosés are made near Metz; *vin gris*, a flinty wine so pale as to be almost beige, is made to the east of Nancy – and also to the west, at Toul, where vineyards destroyed by war have been built up again and produce a little-known red wine as well as the grey.

Toul lies about halfway between Nancy and Domrémy, where Joan of Arc was born. It began as a crossroads town, and still is, with a new motorway running north to south and cars and lorries pouring along on the southern edge on the road from Reims to Nancy. Barges take it easier along the canal that connects the Marne with the Rhine. Toul suffered from both the German advance at the start of the Second World War and General Patton's progress at the end; the stained glass has gone from the fine Gothic cathedral, whose towers are solid from a distance, but a tracery of stone close to. But notwithstanding the wars, the cars and the growth of industry, the centre keeps something of the quiet of the market town.

The Dauphin restaurant is just outside Toul, with green fields through the kitchen windows – for, being a moden building, it is not dedicated to the idea that chefs do not deserve to see the light of day – and it displays its menu by the car park in a kind of glassed-in dolmen with flowers before it, so that it has the air of a roadside shrine. Its high priest, M. Vohmann, cooks perch with local wine, for there is a tradition of eating freshwater fish in this inland province – but, unusually, it is red wine. The fish is simply fried, so the essential part of the recipe is the sauce, which of course can be used with other fish as well. A suitable replacement for the wine of Toul, which you will be unable to get, is something light with a degree of acidity – a red Sancerre is the sort of style – rather than anything fruity or full-bodied. In the absence of fresh chanterelles, a few dried fungi (such as *porcini* from Italian grocers) added to the wine and fish trimmings will give the sauce that touch of the exotic which ordinary mushrooms cannot provide. In spite of its name, concentrated tomato purée does not substitute well for less aggressive and more natural forms of tomato in recipes like this. Mouli fresh tomatoes or canned tomatoes; or cook tomatoes gently until they collapse, and sieve them.

# PERCH WITH RED WINE AND CHANTERELLES

M. VOHMANN, DAUPHIN RESTAURANT, TOUL, LORRAINE

ENOUGH FOR 4 PEOPLE

| |
|---|
| 1 perch weighing about 1 kg (2$\frac{1}{4}$ lb) |
| About 570 ml (1 pint) light red wine |
| 4 shallots, finely chopped |
| About 100 g (4 oz) butter |
| 3 tablespoons fresh tomato purée |
| 4 slices beef marrow |
| 200 g (7 oz) chanterelles, washed and chopped |
| 6 young leeks, sliced thickly |
| Salt and pepper |
| Sugar |
| Juice of $\frac{1}{2}$ lemon |
| Butter for frying |

PREPARATION: Fillet the fish, leaving the skin on (or ask your fishmonger to fillet it for you). Cut it into 4 steaks and dry them on kitchen paper. Bring the fish trimmings to the boil in the wine; turn down the heat and keep the stock just simmering for about 20 minutes.

Lightly fry the shallots in some butter until they are golden, then strain in the stock and add the tomato purée. Leave the sauce to reduce by about two-thirds. Poach the slices of beef marrow for 8 minutes. Cook the leeks and chanterelles for about 5 minutes in separate pans, with butter, a little salt, and a dash of water.

Drain the leeks and chanterelles and add 3 or 4 tablespoons of juice from the chanterelles to the sauce. Season the sauce with salt, pepper, a little sugar and some lemon juice and beat in 2 tablespoons of butter.

Fry the fish in butter until it is golden. Pour the sauce over half of each plate and put the fish on top. Arrange the beef marrow and vegetables on the other side.

# ALSACE

*'Drinking water willy-nilly*
*Makes your stomach really chilly.*
*Don't become a cold collation!*
*Take good wine in moderation.*
*Savour every subtlety —*
*And all the water, leave to me'*
Inscription on a well in Kaysersberg, Alsace

The historic link between Lorraine and Alsace is the Saverne pass, famed for its oversized Rohan palace, and the massacre in 1525 of the *rustauds*, revolutionary peasants who — like Wat Tyler — were unwise enough to trust in the promises of the Establishment. Sometimes in Alsace it has seemed that there is more wine flowing than water, and more blood than wine. It is now an age of wine (and, to go with it, Saverne is famous for its roses); and the water goes uphill — courtesy of the Marne-Rhine canal, where many hours through the locks are now shortened to a few minutes in a gigantic lift which takes the barge, the cargo and the water to float them both.

Half-timbering that was French begins to look German; and there is an increasing tendency for the houses to grow window-boxes, balconies and outside staircases, as if they had ambitions to go on the stage in a romantic costume drama. However fiercely loyal to France Alsace may have been made by German occupation, it is really an in-between, its character formed by the Rhine with its continual flow of merchant traffic. Goethe said that German dough needed French yeast; and both are here, producing all kinds of happy combinations: fruity, fragrant Rhineland wines with French quality and crispness; hostelries which, being halfway between the land of cafés and the land of *Bierkellers*, turn out rather like pubs; and yeast cakes such as *Kugelhopf* (made in the shape of a medieval hat) and *Berawecka* (pear bread), which is eaten after Midnight Mass on Christmas Eve.

The recipe for pear bread given here comes from Eguisheim, a town which is today almost as it was in the sixteenth century, with circles of old houses repeating the pattern of the town walls until they reach the centre, and a ruined castle from the eighth century above — its triple towers traditionally inhabited by witches, one of whom married her daughter to Satan himself. The magic of *Berawecka* worked by Mme Freundenreich — chubby, bespectacled, practical as a pinafore — begins with a more delightful spirit, one of the *alcools blancs* (fruit brandies) for which both sides of the Vosges are celebrated: quetsch and mirabelle (both plum), framboise (raspberry), kirsch (cherry), Poire William (pear). She chose quetsch.

# PEAR BREAD
## (*Berawecka*)
MME FREUNDENREICH, EGUISHEIM, ALSACE

MAKES 2 kg (4½ lb) OF DOUGH (6–8 LOAVES)

| |
|---|
| **500 g (1 lb 2 oz) dried pears** |
| **250 g (9 oz) prunes** |
| **125 g (4½ oz) vanilla sugar** |
| **A large sprinkle of cinnamon** |
| **A sprinkle each of ground cloves, aniseed, salt and pepper** |
| **150 to 275 ml (¼ to ½ pint) fruit brandy** |
| **250 g (9 oz) dried figs, chopped in small pieces** |
| **125 g (4½ oz) raisins, chopped in small pieces** |
| **125 g (4½ oz) candied orange or lemon peel, thinly sliced** |
| **100 g (4 oz) walnuts, thinly sliced** |
| **125 g (4½ oz) hazelnuts, thinly sliced** |
| **250 g (9 oz) blanched almonds, a few left whole for decoration, the rest thinly sliced** |
| **20 g (½ oz) fresh yeast (or 1 heaped teaspoon dried yeast)** |
| **250 g (9 oz) flour (preferably strong flour)** |
| **Sugar and water for glaze** |

PREPARATION: Soak the pears and prunes in a little warm water overnight. Drain them, but keep the water. Chop them in small pieces. Add the sugar and spices to the fruit brandy and marinate all the chopped and sliced fruit and nuts in the brandy for 3 days.

Warm the water the fruits were soaked in and mix it with the yeast. If you are using dried yeast, leave the liquid in a warm place for about 10 minutes, until it is frothy. Mix with the flour as much of the liquid as makes a soft, just manageable dough when you have finished kneading. Put the dough to rise, covered, in a warm place for 1 to 2 hours. When it is well risen, mix in the fruit and nuts with their marinade, distributing the ingredients evenly through the dough. Preheat the oven to 180°C (350°F, gas mark 4). Grease and flour a baking sheet. Form the dough into little loaves 20 to 30 cm (8 to 12 inches) long, roll them in flour and decorate with blanched almonds in the shape of a cross. Bake for 45 to 60 minutes according to size. Brush with a glaze of 1 to 2 tablespoons of sugar dissolved in ½ cup of warm water. Hide the loaves from the family for a week, if you can.

The attractions of Lorraine are half-hidden, waiting for discovery in an orchard, over a green hill, in a mist. Alsace is less ambiguous: it has clarity and contrasts. The winters are colder and longer than in Lorraine, but the summers are hotter and the weather in general is drier. The country does not roll – it descends from the Vosges, a smooth-topped, not a craggy, barrier, often breast-shaped, with castles for nipples. In the forests of dark firs, beech, birch and chestnut are wild raspberries, strawberries, blackberries, mushrooms and game. From the *chaumes* – the summer farms on the high pastures – comes Münster cheese (or Géromé), an open-air cheese that easily takes over more confined spaces. Often eaten with caraway and chopped onion, Münster is said to have been invented by Irish monks three or four centuries before the Norman Conquest. Below the foothills it is plain, with a patchwork of intensive cultivation: walnuts, almonds, peaches ripen in Alsace as they do in Palatinate summers. Between are the towns, the wine road, and hillsides that turn to vines below the much-gabled town of Obernai.

Though the vineyards often went untouched by marauding armies – whose policy, as with the goose that lays the golden egg, was to preserve the grape that makes the golden wine – there is darkness in the history of these sunny towns. The witch of Eguisheim who married her daughter to the devil was a real woman, if not a real witch, and was burned alive. At Le Struthof in the mountains, they have preserved the .vazi concentration camp in memory of ten thousand who died there. Nowadays the locals bounce happily in and out of French, German and their own patois: but the time is not forgotten when French was forbidden – nor is the somewhat bitter laughter in Mulhouse, when the occupiers renamed the main street Adolf Hitler Strasse, unconscious of the irony of the fact that its previous name was Rue du Sauvage.

As any wine-grower knows, some years are good, some bad; and a wine needs not only sweetness but acidity. The Alsatians – who have good heads not only for wine but for realities – have been well taught that life and history are also like that. So, when they read the inscriptions of their ancestors – 'I love the past, good living and good wine' (written up at Kienzheim); 'Mysterious voices breathe into our maturing wine old tales that remain forever young' (painted on a beam above a winepress in Riquewihr) – they understand more than the description of simple pleasure that some tourists see.

Some pleasures are not so much simple as opulent. The most famous dish of Alsace, *pâté de foie gras en croûte*, was created in the eighteenth century by a Norman, Jean-Pierre Close. His materials were not new: for the idea of bloating the liver of a goose – by methods which incline some people to treat the end-product more as a monstrosity than a delicacy – goes back to the Romans: but from then on the pâté-makers of Strasbourg were renowned.

Surely, the establishment of the Council of Europe in Strasbourg can have had nothing at all to do with the international reputation of the Strasbourg restaurants, however happy a coincidence it may be for the Euro-MPs? The quality of the food is simply the logical reward for being in a city that has always stood at the heart of European trade (the 'Stras' in Strasbourg means 'roads'). This recipe for chicken in wine comes from René Britel of the Maison des Tanneurs – so called because the four-centuries-old restaurant is in the former tanners' quarter, La Petite France, a place of bridges over the waterways and old houses which sag in all the most romantic places.

It is the Alsatian version of *Coq au Vin* – *Coq au Riesling*. If you cannot supply the wild mushrooms called for, a combination of ordinary British mushrooms with a few dried *porcini* or the like is a possible substitute.

# CHICKEN IN WHITE WINE
## (*Coq au Riesling*)
RENÉ BRITEL, MAISON DES TANNEURS RESTAURANT, STRASBOURG

ENOUGH FOR 4 PEOPLE

| |
|---|
| 1 medium chicken |
| 200 g (7 oz) butter |
| 2 shallots, chopped |
| 500 ml (17 fl oz) Riesling |
| 150 g (5 oz) each chanterelles and ceps (or ordinary mushrooms with a few dried *porcini*) |
| 2 cloves of garlic, finely chopped |
| 500 ml (17 fl oz) cream |
| Salt and pepper |
| Nutmeg |
| 4 slices of bread |
| Parsley (optional) |
| *White stock* |
| 1 clove of garlic, crushed |
| 1 leek, roughly chopped |
| 1 onion, roughly chopped |
| 1 clove |
| 1 bay leaf |
| A handful of parsley |
| 2 litres ($3\frac{1}{2}$ pints) water |

PREPARATION: If you are using dried mushrooms, put them to soak in warm water. Cut the chicken into 4 pieces – 2 breasts with wings and 2 leg joints – trimming as necessary. Make the stock. Put the chicken trimmings into a pan with the giblets and add the crushed clove of garlic, the leek, onion, clove, bay leaf and parsley and the water. Bring to simmering point and simmer for 30 minutes or more.

Salt and pepper the chicken pieces and brown them in 50 g (2 oz) butter, adding the shallots halfway through. When the chicken pieces are golden brown, pour in the Riesling and strain the stock over. Leave the chicken to cook for 25 minutes.

Prepare the mushrooms as necessary (wild ones may need washing) and cut them up (not too small). Chop the cloves of garlic finely, sweat them in butter and sauté the mushrooms with them.

When the chicken is done, take it out and add the cream to the stock. Reduce the sauce by half and put in the mushrooms. Correct the seasoning with salt, pepper and nutmeg and return the chicken pieces to the sauce.

Fry some croûtons in the remaining butter (at the Maison des Tanneurs the bread is cut into heart shapes whose tips are dipped into chopped parsley). Arrange the mushrooms and chicken pieces on the serving dish and coat the chicken with sauce. Garnish with croûtons. Serve the rest of the sauce separately.

# BURGUNDY

*'Better a good meal than a feast of garments.'* Burgundian proverb

The main difference between a chicken and a *coq* is that a *coq* is what you get on menus, and a chicken is what you can get in a shop. The standard French maize-fed chicken is noticeably superior to the pallid frozen objects at the low end of our market. Some French chickens carry a sort of *appellation contrôlée*, and in Burgundy there is a club of people sworn to eat no other fowl than one that is bred in Bresse.

A French chef will value *un vrai coq* for its (usually rather loosely defined) excellence of flavour. A cock gets tougher earlier than a hen: hence the stewing in recipes created when a chicken was a luxury and would often be a cast-out from the coop; so a *Coq au Riesling*, or, even more so, a *Coq au Vin*, is designed for an older, more flavoursome bird than the usual run of roasting chickens. Look for a good boiling fowl which is not so old as to be stringy.

This recipe from Burgundy specifies half a 3 or 3.5 kg (7 or 8 lb) bird in preference to a whole one younger and smaller. The cooking process is much heartier – and longer – than in the Alsace recipe; as it needs to be to tenderise what may be a monster. Do not try to chop a chicken with something meant for peeling the potatoes: a heavy knife goes through the bones of a hefty chicken far more easily. The red wine sauce garnished with mushrooms and small onions is the classical *à la Bourguignonne* (and in older recipes may be thickened with a liaison of blood). The main problems with it are paying for the wine and peeling the onions, which should be about the size of pickling onions. Chopping off the ends and dropping into boiling water helps with dry-skinned onions, or use overgrown bulbous spring onions.

# CHICKEN IN RED WINE
## (*Coq au Vin*)
### CHÂTEAUNEUF–EN–AUXOIS, BURGUNDY
### ENOUGH FOR 4 PEOPLE

| |
|---|
| **1.25 to 1.75 kg (3 to 4 lb) cock or chicken** |
| **A bottle of substantial (but not extravagant) red wine** |
| **2 medium onions, chopped** |
| **2 cloves of garlic, finely chopped** |
| **2 carrots, diced** |
| **1 bouquet garni containing celery, thyme, parsley and a bay leaf** |
| **Oil for frying** |
| **1 tablespoon flour (optional)** |
| **Salt and pepper** |
| **900 g (2 lb) potatoes, peeled** |
| ***Garnish*** |
| **12 small onions, trimmed** |
| **50 g (2 oz) butter** |
| **100 g (4 oz) smoked fat bacon, cut into strips** |
| **150 g (5 oz) mushrooms, sliced** |

PREPARATION: Chop the bird into 7 cm (3 inch) pieces and put them into a bowl with the onions, garlic, carrots and bouquet garni. Cover with red wine and marinate for 24 hours.

Drain the chicken pieces and brown them in just enough oil; drain the vegetables and add them with a spoon of flour for thickening, if you like (the sauce will reduce greatly during cooking). Pour on the marinade (with the bouquet garni) and simmer uncovered until the chicken is well cooked (2 to 3 hours, depending on the age of the bird), adding salt and pepper to taste.

About an hour before the end, glaze the small onions: cook them slowly with the butter and 4 tablespoons of water (or white stock or wine) in a covered pan, rolling them from time to time until the liquid has all evaporated. This will take up to 45 minutes. The onions should be slightly softened but still with a bit of bite, and they should remain white in colour.

Put the potatoes on to boil or steam, to be ready with the chicken. Fry the bacon pieces in a little oil. When the bacon is almost cooked, add the mushrooms and onions and leave on a low heat for the mushrooms to soften a little.

When the chicken is done, arrange it on the serving dish with the garnish of bacon, onions and mushrooms on top. Strain the sauce over and serve accompanied by the boiled potatoes.

There may be people who cook their *coq* in burgundy, but they cannot be many. The multitude of tiny vineyards that made wine for themselves and for France, then for an international élite, now produces for a world market which – if it knows nothing else – knows the names of Chablis, Beaune, Nuits-St-Georges. There is not enough to go round, and a captive market: the results are predictable. Great burgundies are for the rich, and everything else is expensive, whatever the quality – which ranges from a classic excellence to something which it would not be any sort of sin to use as a *coq*-cooker, were it not so dear.

Despite this, Burgundy has not lost its magic. More a kingdom than a dukedom through much of its history, it was the envy of the courts of the Middle Ages for the flowering of its arts, architecture, manners and religion. It was a court with its roots in the soil; that knew what to value; whose rule was good living. The Burgundian love of life glows from the luxurious paintings, the Romanesque architecture. Elsewhere, impossible traceries of stone speak of the spirit, the intellectual: Romanesque speaks of the body. Its ornament and solidity are right for stone as Burgundian cooking is right for food. It is a country of the body, its energies and its pleasures – and those pleasures include making things well, valuing them for what they are.

Italy: Artichokes with Potatoes page 88

This ancient and gracious prosperity and energy is one reason why Burgundian cooking is the best in France – though not the most pretentious; the other is the fertility and variety of this most pastoral of countrysides, dotted with castles and manor houses whose round towers wear conical roofs like witches' hats.

Above the motorway to Paris, not far from Dijon and closer still to Nuits-St-Georges, Vougeot and Gévrey-Chambertin, is the castle of Châteauneuf-en-Auxois, with rooks round its towers and a red-roofed village in humble attendance. A lane winds to it through a valley of pollarded willows, green meadows and white cows – the Charolais: long, muscular (they were originally draught animals, like the heavy horses for which Auxois was famous), and good beef. The cooking in Châteauneuf has improved considerably since the fifteenth-century *châtelaine* Catherine was executed for attempting to feed poisoned cakes to her husband. She should have made Pear Charlotte, a pudding it is quite impossible for anyone to refuse.

There are basically two kinds of charlotte: charlotte russe, Bavarian cream within a palisade of alcohol-soaked sponge fingers, eaten cold; and fruit charlotte, fruit mixture enclosed by slices of bread and butter, baked in the oven and usually served hot. This charlotte has the cream of one with the fruit of the other. Needless to say, Burgundy fruit is celebrated (like everything else in the province), particularly the Bigarreaux cherries of Yonne (which Cockney costers used to cry as 'Bigaroons'), and the blackcurrants of Dijon, which go to make the cordial cassis. Pear Charlotte has some of the qualities of a trifle, but greater sophistication. It is pretty heavy on the alcohol, the inimitably fragrant (and expensive) Poire William, but it is not the same without it. The quantities given here are for a 26 cm (10 inch) diameter mould: if you use a smaller one, you will need to reduce the quantities proportionately, as well as the number of pear quarters used on the garnish.

Portugal: Salt Cod à·Bras page 97

# PEAR CHARLOTTE

CHÂTEAUNEUF–EN–AUXOIS, BURGUNDY

ENOUGH FOR 12 PEOPLE

| |
|---|
| **800 g (1¾ lb) granulated sugar** |
| **1 litre (1¾ pints) water** |
| **12 pears** |
| **50 g (2 oz) powdered milk** |
| **A few drops of vanilla essence or half a vanilla pod** |
| **10 leaves of gelatine or 4 packets powdered gelatine** |
| **10 eggs, separated** |
| **250 ml (9 fl oz) Poire William** |
| **570 ml (1 pint) double cream** |
| **250 g (9 oz) caster sugar** |
| **About 14 sponge-finger biscuits** |
| **Apricot jam** |
| **Redcurrant jelly** |
| **You will also need a flan ring 26 cm (10 inch) diameter × 5 cm (2 inches) deep** |

PREPARATION: Dissolve 700 g (1½ lb) sugar in 1 litre (1¾ pints) water, and boil hard for 1 minute. Reduce the heat and keep the syrup at a gentle simmer while you peel the pears. Halve all except one, which should also retain its stalk. Simmer the pears in the syrup until they are tender but not darkened. This will probably take about 30 minutes. Lift the pears out of the syrup. Add the powdered milk and the vanilla to 750 ml (1¼ pints) of the pear syrup, bring it to the boil and leave it to simmer. (Powdered milk is used to avoid diluting the pear syrup with liquid milk.) Dissolve the gelatine as directed on the packet.

Mix the egg yolks with the remaining granulated sugar in a saucepan. Off the heat, stir in the hot syrup mixture. Still stirring, heat gently for a minute or two to make a light custard (be careful to keep it off the boil). Strain the custard into a bowl and add the gelatine. Put the custard in the refrigerator. When it is thoroughly chilled, stir in two-thirds of the Poire William.

Whip the cream till stiff. Mix 4 egg whites with the caster sugar and beat them over hot water to make a meringue that holds a peak. Keep a little whipped cream back to decorate the top of the charlotte. Fold the rest of the cream into the custard, then fold in the meringue.

Assemble the charlotte. Put the rest of the Poire William in a bowl and add pear syrup to taste. Put the flan ring on to the serving dish. Cut the halved pears into quarters lengthways. One by one, dip the sponge fingers in the Poire William and syrup mixture and line the sides of the flan ring with them. Put a layer of cream filling at the bottom with 8 pear quarters on top, then pile in the rest of the filling. Smooth the top and arrange the rest of the pear quarters on it like the spokes of a wheel, with the whole pear standing in the middle.

Glaze the pears by brushing them with some apricot jam melted with a little water. Melt some redcurrant jelly and pour a little down the gaps between the biscuits (or some of them). Decorate with whirls of whipped cream. Refrigerate for 12 hours before serving.

A story for which I cannot vouch, but which is quoted by no less an authority than *Larousse Gastronomique*, is that there is a hotel in Dijon with wine taps in its bedrooms. Certainly, Burgundy's capital with its renowned International Food Fair is as central to the world of food – and drink – as the stuffing is in a turkey. Dijon is famous for two products in particular. At its best, cassis (or *crème de cassis*) is a subtle and alcoholic blackcurrant cordial. It is really a ratafia – and making it at home is only a matter of mixing blackcurrants, sugar and alcohol in some form, usually brandy, and leaving it to mature for several weeks. It was made by generations of peasants before it was mass-produced and marketed. Its reputation is that it is just about the only thing you can mix with a good white wine without removing all dignity from the wine. Kir, as a cocktail of cassis and white burgundy is called, is named after Canon Kir, the post-war Deputy and Mayor of Dijon, a national personality who popularised the drink, promoting cassis and white burgundies at the same time. (There are no commercial flies on the Burgundians.) His other memorial is a large recreation lake; and certain people would quite happily see his fashionable aperitif dumped in it. They are those who have been served a good white wine turned into a childhood catastrophe by the addition of too much cassis; or a bad white wine which someone thought they could use up by doctoring it. Kir has a certain summer charm, but it needs a reasonable (not an extravagant) dry white wine (well chilled) and enough of the best cassis to tinge it: it will take a little more blackcurrant if you add a few drops of angostura.

The thing that Dijon makes that nobody can do without is its mustard, which is simple enough but, somehow, nothing else is quite the same in a salad dressing – and it should be the common-or-garden ground yellow mustard, not the whole-seed *à l'ancienne*.

Dijon has been fortunately situated — far enough from Paris to be independent, but not so distant as to be in the sticks; and when it was about to be bypassed by the railway in the nineteenth century, the local fixers moved heaven and earth to get the route changed. Burgundian food is similarly placed: the apotheosis of provincial cooking, it does not seek technical virtuosity for its own sake, but cooks its fare in the very best way it can think of, pleasing both good amateur cooks and Rabelaisian eaters.

The good raw materials of Burgundy are so many that the range of the menu is a study in itself: but among them are snails. The British can never understand why the French eat snails, but one reason is that they are exceedingly common in vineyards (unless killed off by chemicals). In France, you have to be careful about gathering snails: the snails on someone's land belong to them and them only, as if they were livestock. I know of no legal actions for snail theft in Britain.

The so-called 'edible' snail, *Helix pomatia*, is a reasonably-sized mouthful (though a pygmy compared to tropical snails which grow to over a foot long) and comes prettily garnished with a banded brown shell. But the black garden snail, *Helix aspersa*, and any land snail, is edible with no more than mental qualms, except in the rather unlikely circumstance that it has just been browsing on something poisonous to you. It is because of this that the snails you collect from the hedgerows after a shower of rain are traditionally isolated in a bucket for between three days and a week with only flour or lettuce leaves to feed on. Some French writers have even advocated starving the hapless creatures for up to a month, which produces on the snails the same sort of effect as it would on you and me: it makes them small and tough. (It probably also makes them bad-tempered, but it is difficult to tell with snails: nor is it easy to work out how you starve them in winter, when they are in hibernation.)

In fact, I understand (from the Snail Centre, Colwyn Bay) that it is not necessary to starve or isolate any snail. They should be plunged into boiling water to kill them, as is sometimes done with shellfish, and dunked up and down a few times to get rid of the worst of the dirt. Generally-quoted cooking times are excessive at three hours or even more: one-and-a-quarter hours is ample. The snails will generally come out of their shells by themselves, when it is easy to see and cut out the visceral hump, the part of the digestive system where the rubbish collects. However, tinned snails can be had in Britain ready prepared: and it is these that are assumed in the next recipe.

Burgundian snail dishes, particularly the classic garlic butter with shallot and parsley, are celebrated. This recipe for a snail fricassee, from Jean-Pierre Billoux of the Dijon Hôtel de la Cloche, is less usual.

# FRICASSEE OF BURGUNDY SNAILS

JEAN-PIERRE BILLOUX, HÔTEL DE LA CLOCHE, DIJON, BURGUNDY

ENOUGH FOR 4 PEOPLE

| |
|---|
| 1 carrot |
| 1 large potato |
| About 75 g (3 oz) butter, at room temperature |
| 4 dozen cooked snails |
| 1 branch of tarragon |
| Juice of $\frac{1}{2}$ lemon (optional) |
| *Court-bouillon* |
| 2 rashers of streaky bacon |
| Butter for frying |
| 1 onion, thinly sliced |
| 1 clove of garlic, crushed |
| 1 carrot, thinly sliced |
| A bottle of dry white wine |
| Salt and pepper |
| 1 sprig of thyme |
| 1 bay leaf |
| 1 branch of tarragon |

PREPARATION: To make the court-bouillon, put the bacon to fry in a little butter, add the onion, the garlic and the sliced carrot, then put in the white wine, salt and pepper, the thyme, the bay leaf and a stalk of tarragon. Leave to simmer gently, uncovered.

Peel the whole carrot and the potato and cut them into long lozenges, or any other elegant shape you fancy. Put the carrot pieces to cook in a little water and butter in one pan, the potato pieces to brown in butter in another.

Put the snails to simmer for 15 minutes in the court-bouillon while you chop the remaining stalk of tarragon with 50 g (2 oz) butter to make tarragon butter. Take the bacon slices from the court-bouillon, cut them across into strips and leave them aside.

When the 15 minutes are up, transfer the snails to another pan and strain the court-bouillon (now well reduced) over them. Add the chopped bacon and the tarragon butter, stirring well, then the pieces of potato and carrot (and, if you like, a squeeze of lemon). Serve hot.

*'Nothing significant exists under Italy's sun that is not touched by art. Its food is twice blessed because it is the product of two arts – the art of cooking and the art of eating.'* Marcella Hazan

When Tosca sings in her most famous aria that she has lived for art, she has lived for love, she sings for all Italy. Italians do well what they love dearly: thus they are good at fast cars, beautiful clothes and food – and awful at bureaucracy. As for art, I remember a hairdresser's assistant in Genoa who was getting married, and preparing her bottom drawer: its proudest feature was an encyclopedia of painting and sculpture.

Historic art remains part of the present. You turn a corner in Rome, and there is something suddenly, wonderfully ancient on whose steps Diocletian probably passed the time of day; all mixed up with flats and crowds and shopping streets and markets. It is inconceivable that the Italians could ever have been Romans, that cool, forbidding race of organisers: for, putting aside the Vatican and the short-lived aberration of Mussolini and his Fascists, they have learned how to value existence on a smaller scale. Perhaps this has come through their centuries of fragmentation into comparatively little kingdoms which have sometimes been glorious and sometimes chaos. The country remains intensely regional.

You would expect a country which has been at the roots, the routes, and the rebirth of Western civilisation to have learned to cook; and the food is one of the great pleasures of the amiable frenzy of Italian life. Among the things that make it so are the regionalism and a food distribution system that has not sold out to those culinary empires, the big food marketeers, but which has kept the small shop, the small restaurant, the small grower and distributor. The length of experience is another factor – they have been in the kitchen a long time, with riches to reach them skill and variety, and poverty to give common sense and respect for simplicity. The result is an almost total lack of food snobbery: in this, Italian cooking is refreshingly different from the French cuisine, which Italian chefs rocked in its cradle.

One of the first printed cookery books was Italian – *De Honesta Voluptate* by Bartolommeo de' Sacchi, published around 1474. Honest voluptuaries are what the Italians still are. They luxuriate in life, and – for all their love of consumer goods when they can afford them – they luxuriate particularly in the simplicities. Italy is a country which is not about its land but about its people. It is this which ensures that no one who has ever been in love with life can fail to love Italy; and which makes the food practical, tasty and so, so transportable.

# SOUTH AND NORTH – NAPLES AND LOMBARDY

*'The angels in Paradise eat nothing but* vermicelli al pomodoro.' The Duke of Bovino, Mayor of Naples, quoted by Elizabeth David

The spaghetti with a tomatoey sauce which is the standard presentation of pasta outside Italy and a frequent one within is an astonishingly international dish in its origins as well as its present-day empire – far wider than anything Julius Caesar ever dreamed of.

The list of shapes of pasta is vast, but the basic ingredient is always the same: very strong flour, made from coarsely milled durum wheat. They love noodles in China, and China is one of the places in the world older than Italy, so perhaps pasta did come from there – even if the recipe was not actually stolen from a Chinese courtesan by a member of Marco Polo's expedition by the name of Signor Spaghetti. But this hard winter wheat grows all round the Mediterranean and pasta's origins may lie much closer to hand. The variety of pasta shapes is not pure novelty, incidentally. The essence of pasta is its shape, which determines the relationship of pasta to flavour by picking up more or less sauce.

The tomato came from the New World during the sixteenth century, and was the Peruvian Apple, the Golden Apple and the Love Apple before the British and a good many other people decided to call it a tomato, from the Mexican name. The older European names have dropped out of use except in Italy, which was the first nation to take the *pomodoro* to its stomach, at a time when others considered it poisonous. The big Mediterranean tomatoes are extremely juicy and eaten very ripe. They are not the only delicious tomatoes in the world, but the glasshouse ones offered to the British public are most often a tasteless hymn to commercialism and a disgrace to the art of gardening: when you are forced to use them, increase the quantity to try to get a bit of flavour – a small pinch of sugar sometimes helps, as well.

Do not confuse tomato sauce with the Bolognese beef-based sauce, which comes from a rich part of Italy noted for its opulent cooking. This tomato sauce is from Naples, where the washing hangs out over the streets like flags, where thieves steal in style, and where many people have been very poor for a very long time. Naples is pasta for the same reason that London was ale –

the unique quality of the water. Since at the time these reputations were made both were outstandingly dirty places, it is perhaps best not to enquire further.

This sauce is particularly for spaghetti, and its only extravagance is a slice of butter and a tiny amount of bacon. But with really good tomatoes and fresh basil, I think it suits pasta better than Bolognese sause. If fresh basil (or frozen) is not to be had, I would never substitute dried basil but use another fresh herb. Always buy a piece of Parmesan cheese in preference to ready grated, if you can.

Never overcook pasta. Cook it in a really ample pan of boiling salted water and test frequently to see whether it has become *al dente*, just biteable. Drain it as soon as it reaches that crucial point, and serve it immediately.

# SPAGHETTI WITH TOMATO SAUCE
### A NAPLES HOUSEWIFE
### ENOUGH FOR 4 PEOPLE

| |
|---|
| **450 g (1 lb) dry spaghetti (or other pasta, fresh or dry)** |
| **75 g (3 oz) butter** |
| **25 g (1 oz) *pancetta* or fat bacon, chopped small** |
| **$\frac{1}{2}$ onion, chopped small** |
| **600 g ($1\frac{1}{4}$ lb) fresh tomatoes, peeled, de-seeded and chopped** |
| **Salt and pepper** |
| **12 or more large leaves of fresh basil, roughly chopped** |
| **75 g (3 oz) Parmesan cheese, grated** |

PREPARATION: Boil a large pot of water, salt it and put in the spaghetti. The sauce will cook in the time it takes to do the spaghetti (usually 12 to 18 minutes for dry spaghetti).

Melt 50 g (2 oz) butter in a saucepan and fry the chopped bacon and onion lightly. Add the tomatoes and season with salt and pepper. Cook gently for 5 minutes or so (not forgetting to check the spaghetti). When the spaghetti is *al dente*, drain it and put it in a hot serving dish with a few pieces of butter. Toss it with the basil, cheese and sauce.

Pasta has a flavour of its own, which should always complement the sauce, rather than be swamped by it. Treat pasta as something to improvise with: melted butter, olive oil and cream are its fats and fresh tastes complement it well. Do not work too hard – the essence and great virtue of much Italian cooking is its speed and simplicity. The simplest sauce of all – butter and fresh herbs, perhaps with raw eggs – is one of the best. Another easy dressing for spaghetti is a cup of olive oil in which two or three hot red peppers broken into pieces have been heated with two crushed whole cloves of garlic. The garlic should not be allowed to colour. The peppers and garlic are left in the oil in which the spaghetti is tossed.

In the heaven cited by the Mayor of Naples it is only southern angels who concentrate on pasta: northern angels traditionally prefer polenta (cornmeal) and rice. These latter angels are better off, and have been so for centuries – for, if there is any simple division of Italy, it is between north and south of a line drawn through Rome. The north – closer to the rest of Europe and with more fertile and amenable country – has always been more prosperous. This imbalance has brought the southern angels in flocks to the great factories of the north, blurring old distinctions and causing the usual resentment. But the food of Piedmont and Lombardy is of such long-standing quality and rich variety that there is no fear that it will fade away.

Piedmont is rather French in style. In Turin, you often hear French in the streets (and the citizens have a not un-Gallic reputation for being stuck-up). Lombardy is also sophisticated and European, but nearby Venice and the cities of the plain of the river Po root it more firmly in Italy. There is a rich variety of ingredients from lake, plain, mountain, pasture and paddy; but even the inhabitants of such a rich industrial city as Milan retain an Italian respect for comparative simplicity.

Milanese risotto (which with *ossobuco* – stewed shin of veal – is the traditional Sunday lunch in that city) is said to have acquired its yellow colouring in 1574 from the hand of a young craftsman working on the stained-glass windows for the ornate cathedral due to be consecrated three years later. He was nicknamed 'Saffron', from his habit of including a pinch in his colourings; and on the wedding day of his master's daughter did the same for the risotto. Turmeric will colour your rice more cheaply, but will not give you the saffron flavour.

Italian rice (cultivated at least since the sixteenth century) is medium-grain – halfway between the pudding sort and the long-grain *basmati*; and risotto is cooked by a method which is a cross between the Indian way of boiling it dry and the slosh-it-about-in-a-lot-of-water school. This risotto was made by a large chef with a lugubrious moustache in a risotto-coloured restaurant in Milan, once a farm but now a lone survival of the countryside in the midst of flats and skyscrapers.

# MILANESE RISOTTO
## A CHEF WITH A DROOPY MOUSTACHE, MILAN
### ENOUGH FOR 4 PEOPLE

| |
|---|
| $\frac{1}{2}$ teaspoon powdered saffron or 1 teaspoon filaments |
| 1 litre (1$\frac{3}{4}$ pints) chicken stock |
| 100 g (3$\frac{1}{2}$ oz) butter |
| 10 g ($\frac{1}{2}$ oz) beef marrow, chopped |
| 1 onion, finely chopped |
| A glass of dry white wine |
| 350 g ($\frac{3}{4}$ lb) Italian rice |
| Salt |
| 3 to 4 tablespoons grated Parmesan cheese |

PREPARATION: Dissolve the saffron powder (or crush and soak filaments) in 275 ml ($\frac{1}{2}$ pint) of stock.

Melt half the butter in a heavy saucepan, add the beef marrow and onion and fry over a moderately brisk heat until the onion is golden, but not brown. Add the white wine and cook to reduce by half.

Stir in the rice, add a little salt (unless the stock will provide enough), and continue cooking and stirring for a minute or two. Cook over a brisk heat, putting in the stock ladle by ladle as the rice absorbs it, stirring very frequently and adding the saffron stock towards the end, after about 20 minutes. Your aim is to get to the point at which the rice is cooked *al dente*, with just enough moisture to make the rice flow, rather than fall, from the pan when you turn it out. But before you do that, stir in the remainder of the butter and the Parmesan, and rest the saucepan off the heat for a minute.

*Ossobuco* is a 5 cm (2 inch) slice cut across the shin of veal, including the bone and its marrow. It is braised slowly with chopped vegetables and tomato in a covered pan on the hob, or it can be done in the oven at not more than 180°C (350°F, gas mark 4) for a couple of hours. Usually *gremolata*, a garnish of lemon zest, garlic and parsley, is added at the end; but some prefer to leave it out. This *ossobuco* was made by a bony chef with a brisk moustache in the same risotto-coloured restaurant.

# BRAISED SHIN OF VEAL
## (*Ossobuco alla Milanese*)
A CHEF WITH A BRISK MOUSTACHE, MILAN

ENOUGH FOR 4 PEOPLE

| |
| --- |
| 4 × 5 cm (2 inch) slices of shin of veal |
| A little flour |
| 50 g (2 oz) butter |
| 1 onion, 1 carrot, 1 stick of celery, finely chopped |
| 3 cloves of garlic, finely chopped |
| Marjoram (fresh or dried) |
| Salt and pepper |
| Grated rind of $1\frac{1}{2}$ lemons |
| 250 ml (9 fl oz) dry white wine |
| 1 large Mediterranean tomato, peeled and chopped |
| 250 ml (9 fl oz) stock |
| A handful of parsley, chopped |

PREPARATION: Flour the pieces of meat and brown them in half the butter in a large pan. Add the chopped onion, carrot and celery and one of the chopped cloves of garlic and fry till the onion is golden, seasoning with marjoram, salt, pepper and the rind of $\frac{1}{2}$ lemon. Pour in the wine and continue to cook until it has reduced by three-quarters.

Add the tomato and the stock and cook, covered, on a very low heat for about $1\frac{1}{2}$ hours, or until the meat is very tender and the sauce well reduced. Mix the remaining chopped garlic and lemon rind with the parsley to make *gremolata*, and add it to the pan with the rest of the butter. Cook covered for a few minutes more.

The veal of Italy is a revelation in flavour; and so are local fruit and vegetables bought fresh from the ground or off the tree or vine in a sunny market. Vegetables seldom get the respect they deserve, even from the best cuisines (and certainly not from many vegetarians in my experience, who often seem to subscribe to Oscar Wilde's dictum that 'Each man kills the thing he loves', and where they do not slaughter the pig, murder the sprouts). Things are improving in our own nation of gardeners, which therefore ought to be also a nation of great vegetable-cooks – and perhaps will be, one day. The Italians are a nation of cultivators, and they already behave fairly nicely to the veg.

They give a place of honour to the salad. As well as individual salad vegetables – those we would regard as everyday and some, such as the red cabbage-like, faintly bitter *radicchio*, which are less familiar – markets sell salad mixtures, a whole crop of different kinds of greens grown together and cut off long before their prime. The proportion of oil to vinegar in a dressing seems to increase as you go south; and the taste of fine olive oil mixes with the sun in the vegetables and herbs to make salads which are the same sort of experience as getting crushed against an Italian momma in the rush hour – no sharp edges to speak of, but a certain piquancy, nevertheless.

The relationships between freshness, crispness, acidity and oiliness are the key to salad-making: which, in the end, depends on the taste of the individual and the quality of the ingredients. Good olive oil, the best Dijon mustard, good wine vinegar, freshly ground black pepper accumulate quality. If you have them all, then a liberal hand with the oil, mustard and pepper should ensure the success of the dressing, at least. Always support good olive oil – if for no other reason than that it comes from the tree of peace (so called because it took years to come to full bearing, and was planted by those who could look forward to an untroubled time). Olive oil varies from the light-flavoured yellow (which I particularly associate with Tuscany) to extremely pungent (which in my mind says 'Spain!') and through several qualities. These qualities (which include the otherwise unknown distinction 'Extra Virgin') chronicle the stages of extraction from the first simple pressing till the time when the strongest persuasions of heat (and, sometimes, chemicals) have to be applied to get anything else out of the fruit. For years I have used a Greek oil which is thick, green and of a substantial but not too dominant flavour.

Dress all salads at the last moment, except those like potato and tomato where the dressing should have a chance to soak in. Always use a lot of dressing, dry ingredients (especially lettuce) before dressing them, go easy on the onion or garlic, and add fresh herbs, the king of which is basil, when you can; and your life will be happy and your memory as green as the salad. But your salad will not taste like mine, nor mine yours – nor either of them like these three salads as made by two brother chefs from the Po Delta. I am aghast at the quantity of onion in the first recipe: I would need a bulb of exceptional sweetness to use so much myself, or blanch the rings for twenty seconds in boiling water. But a salad is an individual matter. I hardly ever bother to de-seed tomatoes, for instance, but de-seeding is more necessary with the large Mediterranean kind, because they are so juicy that they dilute the dressing.

The second salad contains cooked vegetables bound with mayonnaise, like Russian salad – but its other fresh ingredients and the capers make it much livelier in both texture and taste. The Red, Green and Orange Salad is more than a contrast in colours, it also has interesting variations in textures; and its flavours, verging on bitterness, need no vinegar to stand against the olive oil. If you cannot get *radicchio*, chicory would provide a similar flavour, though a different texture and colour.

# PO DELTA SALAD
TWO BROTHERS, PO DELTA

ENOUGH FOR 4 PEOPLE

| |
|---|
| 4 large tomatoes, skinned, de-seeded and sliced |
| 2 cold boiled potatoes, sliced |
| 1 celery stalk, very thinly sliced |
| 1 medium onion, thinly sliced |
| 2 hard-boiled eggs, sliced |
| 2 tablespoons vinegar |
| 2 to 3 heaped teaspoons French mustard |
| Salt and pepper |
| 7 to 8 tablespoons olive oil |

PREPARATION: Arrange the tomatoes in the bottom of the bowl, make a layer of potato slices above them, scatter the celery over, and cover with onion rings. Finish with the eggs on top.

Mix the vinegar, mustard and salt in a bowl. Stir in the oil, then the pepper. Pour over the salad and allow it to steep. Toss once just before serving.

# FANTASY SALAD
TWO BROTHERS, PO DELTA

ENOUGH FOR 4 PEOPLE

| |
|---|
| 4 big Mediterranean-type tomatoes |
| 2 celery stalks, finely chopped |
| A handful of cooked green beans, chopped |
| 2 tablespoons cooked peas |
| 1 carrot, grated |
| 2 tablespoons capers |
| 3 tablespoons mayonnaise |
| Salt and pepper (optional) |

PREPARATION: Cut the tops off the tomatoes and scoop out the middles. Mix all the rest of the salad ingredients together, correct the seasoning if necessary, stuff the tomatoes, and serve cool.

# RED, GREEN AND ORANGE SALAD

TWO BROTHERS, PO DELTA

ENOUGH FOR 4 PEOPLE

| |
|---|
| **3 oranges, peeled and sliced** |
| **1 *radicchio*, in 5 cm (2 inch) slices** |
| **1 lettuce heart, leaves separated** |
| **Olive oil** |
| **Salt and pepper** |

PREPARATION: Arrange in layers – orange, *radicchio*, lettuce – and border with orange slices. Dress with plenty of well-seasoned olive oil.

## SICILY AND SARDINIA
*Bitter honey*

South of Rome, the land of the midday sun – the Mezzogiorno – gets wilder as it goes further south. From the days of Rome it has been underprivileged: Caesar's officers were rewarded with estates further north, while the malarial south was settled by slaves. Furthest south of all is Sicily, with a reputation for being poor and dishonest – but with a richness in its past that marks it off from Italy's other big island, Sardinia.

Sardinia is an outpost where Sicily is a hub: for, though Sicily may be at the toe of the boot, it is central to the Mediterranean. The islands share a great talent for being invaded, often by the same people, but where the Sicilian invasions included cultures, the Sardinian were mostly soldiers; and the Sards have never lost a touch of cragginess which perhaps goes back to their earliest forefathers, who left the landscape strewn with mysterious towers, the *nuraghi*.

Both islands have a reputation for lawlessness; but it is lawlessness of very different kinds. The Sicilian *mafioso* is a fixer, who exploits the poor on the basis of reprisal – an alternative and corrupt Establishment. A bandit is an outlaw, and the people do not usually regard him as an enemy. 'No brigands here', they say in Sardinia, '– and very nice people too.' They stand for natural justice, while the *mafioso* is for natural injustice. The great figure of Sardinia is not an emperor, like Dionysius of Sicily, not a mythological figure like Cyclops or Hercules, not a philosopher like Empedocles, but Eleonora, the Sardinian Joan of Arc, who gave the island laws and a brief respite in a long history of exploitation and injustice.

There is much in common between the cooking of the islands, which includes a taste for sweet things (though Sardinia is noted for its *miele amaro*, bitter honey); but it seems appropriate to take an elaborate cake from Sicily and a peasant dish from Sardinia.

The most unexpected invasions of Sicily were of Normans (who have left an occasional strain of Nordic blondness among the dark-haired southerners) and of Germans (one of whom, the Emperor Frederick II, created an illustrious court); but among the most influential voyagers over the wine-dark seas of Homer were Arabs, who ruled for two centuries, and left behind them a tradition of decoration and a taste for sweetmeats.

Sicilian carts are famous – decorated as our Romany caravans are, but with much greater elaboration; and the style spills over into confectionery, which makes figures of horses and men which no Greek god would sniff at as a votive offering. This Sicilian *cassata* is not an ice cream but an uncooked cheesecake. It is made with ricotta, but if you cannot find this, other soft cheeses can be used instead – for example, a mixture of cottage cheese and cream cheese – or something like a thick vanilla cream or even ice cream. Candied peel is not the best substitute for the pumpkin, because the texture is a bit tough against the cheese; something softer would be better.

The main interest of this cake is in the construction, which allows you to enclose a soft filling. The sides may be made entirely of marzipan or – as here – of both marzipan and sponge. The shape is formed in a circular mould with the sides sloping in towards the bottom (these quantities being for one 16 cm (6¼ inches) across and 3 cm (1¼ inches) deep). It might be as well to allow yourself a little extra sponge and marzipan the first time. At the end, the decoration is extremely heavy on candied fruit. If you feel you are overdoing it, you are probably beginning to approach authenticity. However, if you prefer, you can leave out the chocolate chips.

# SICILIAN CASSATA
## A CONFECTIONERY FACTORY IN SICILY
### SERVES 4

| |
|---|
| 300 g (11 oz) ricotta cheese |
| 100 g (4 oz) caster sugar |
| 50 g (2 oz) candied pumpkin, chopped |
| 50 g (2 oz) plain chocolate chips (optional) |
| 100 g (4 oz) marzipan |
| 100 g (4 oz) sponge cake (in an oblong slab, not a round) |
| 150 g (5 oz) mixed crystallised fruit |
| *Fondant icing* |
| 500 g (1 lb) sugar |
| 150 ml ($\frac{1}{4}$ pint) water |
| A pinch of cream of tartar |
| A few drops of lemon or orange essence |

PREPARATION: Make the icing first. Dissolve the sugar in the water, add the cream of tartar, bring the syrup to the boil and boil it for 2 to 3 minutes, to the soft ball stage. (To test, drop a little into cold water, then immediately fish it out. If it forms a lump that you are able to roll into a ball between your fingers, it has reached the soft ball stage.) Sprinkle some cold water on to a cool work surface and pour the hot syrup on to it. Leave it to cool slightly, work it with a palette knife until it becomes thick and white, then knead it well. Wrap it in foil until you are ready to use it.

To make the filling, mix the cheese with the sugar. Sieve the mixture if it is at all uneven in texture. Stir in the chopped pumpkin and the chocolate pieces.

Flour the mould lightly. Roll the marzipan and cut the sponge cake into strips rather deeper than the mould. Cut the strips into vertical sections that are slightly narrower at one end than the other (to allow for the fact that the mould narrows at the bottom). Line the sides of the mould with alternate pieces of marzipan and sponge. Roll a long, thin sausage of marzipan with your hands and lay it round the bottom edge, pressing it to bind it to the sponge and marzipan sides. Line the base of the tin with sponge. Trim the top edge level with the top of the mould. Fill tightly to the top with the cheese mixture and cover the top with pieces of sponge. Put a cake base or a plate on the mould and, holding mould and plate firmly together, turn them over. Press down on the mould and lift it off.

Put the fondant icing in a bowl set over a pan of hot water. When it begins to melt, stir in the lemon or orange essence. Continue to stir until the icing has the consistency of thick cream. Ice the *cassata*. Allow the icing to harden, then decorate the cake extravagantly with crystallised fruits arranged in a four-leaved clover pattern.

~~ • ~~

The Sardinian dish – a vegetarian main course – was made by a girl of Solarussa, a village not far from Oristano, which boasts the best that Sardinia can do in the way of flat land at the seaward end of the Tirso valley. Sardinia is celebrated for its *amaretti* (almond biscuits of the bitter-sweetness all Italians love), *accarraxiau* (sucking pig done up in a sheep's stomach, then roasted in a hole in the ground) and *taccula* (a dish of blackbirds or thrushes); and for its globe artichokes.

Like the tomato, the artichoke spread to Europe through Italy, via the tables of the nobility. It is a creature of implicit refinement: eating an artichoke is like courtship – it takes time, involves a number of stages of undressing, a certain amount of teasing; and the *pièce de résistance* is the bottom.

The Sardinian dish of artichokes with potatoes given here is extremely simple and deceptively modest – chunks of potato with quartered artichokes (leaves and all) cooked with olive oil, onion and tomato. The taste begins by being unassuming, but you find yourself coming back for more as you realise what a happy combination it is. The better each of the simple ingredients, the happier. Good olive oil is critical. Getting well-flavoured tomatoes should not present too much difficulty, since even if the only fresh ones available taste of nothing but artificial light and oversized greenhouses, good tinned ones are quite acceptable in this dish. Artichokes are more of a problem: even now, they are unfamiliar – and even mysterious – vegetables to many people.

There are many reasons for this, which begin with the fact that we use the same name for two totally different vegetables – the knobbly Jerusalem artichoke, which is an ugly tuber, and the globe artichoke, which is a thistle flower. The best bit of a globe artichoke is its bottom (the thick disc inside the base of the leaves); and how much you can eat of the area around it depends on the age and freshness. If it is quite a bit younger and smaller than we find in British shops, the artichoke can be eaten entire. As it develops, the choke (the nest of fibres on top of the bottom) becomes more and more choking and always has to be discarded. The leaves harden from the top down and the outside in, until – in an older artichoke – the only edible parts are the bottom and the fleshy insides of the bottoms of the leaves, which are usually dipped in vinaigrette or hollandaise sauce and scraped off against the teeth.

Artichokes are nearly always cooked, but it is possible to eat the best parts of a young one raw – even the stalk, provided that you cut away the tough outer skin. It tastes crisp and vegetable-like.

For this dish, buy the smallest artichokes you can find, trim the stalks to 2.5 cm (1 inch) long and peel them upwards, removing the small leaves at the base of the flower. Then you have to remove the choke, strip enough of the tough outer leaves and cut off enough of the tips of the remaining ones to give you hope that you have got rid of most of the stringy bits. (What is enough to cut off depends on that particular artichoke.) Halving or quartering the artichokes lengthways, as in this dish, makes it much easier to take out the choke fibres but reveals a tendency to discolour at astonishing speed, so as soon as you have prepared them put them into a bowl of water with a little lemon juice or vinegar. And don't cook them in an aluminium pan.

Artichoke bottoms alone, fresh or tinned, can be used; and if you hate artichokes anyway, this is quite a nice way of just doing potatoes. Sardinia's Vernaccia wine, dry, white and delicate, comes from nearby, but is much too up-market for such humble food.

# ARTICHOKES WITH POTATOES
A GIRL FROM SOLARUSSA

ENOUGH FOR 4 PEOPLE

| |
|---|
| **9 small globe artichokes** |
| **6 medium potatoes, cubed** |
| **1 large onion, chopped** |
| **Olive oil for frying** |
| **Salt and pepper** |
| **6 tomatoes, peeled and chopped** |
| **A handful of parsley, finely chopped** |

PREPARATION: Prepare the artichokes as described above, quarter them, and keep them in acidulated water.

Fry the onion in oil until it is beginning to soften. Drain and dry the artichokes and toss them well with the onion for a minute or two. Season with salt and pepper. Add the tomatoes and the potatoes. Continue simmering and stirring until the tomatoes are beginning to go mushy. Mix in the chopped parsley. Add about half as much water as would cover, put the lid on the pan and simmer until the potatoes are cooked. Stir from time to time, correct the seasoning and add more water, or uncover the pan to reduce the sauce, as necessary. At the end, the sauce should be concentrated rather than liquid (though a weaker broth is also quite pleasant).

# PORTUGAL

*An exciting chapter containing an Earthquake, Red-hot Irons, Nun's Nipples and the Battle of the Chef Horácio with a Codfish*

The Portuguese are Atlantic independents: they are also Mediterranean Catholics. So they like to have miracles in their country: one of them happens regularly in the white-tiled kitchen of Dona Amélia, who lives in Leça da Palmeira, near Oporto.

Frankly, it is not much of a miracle. It is more of a ritual. But it is a tiny revelation.

Dona Amélia works in a restaurant that overlooks the sea, with tangly glass tanks of crabs and lobsters in its larder. She has just got out her red-hot irons, which are coming up to temperature nicely on the gas – heavy discs of metal flopping around on long handles. With a discreet flourish, she picks one up and applies it to the first of a tray of inoffensive milk puddings resting, belly-upwards, in their bowls. Smoke rises like the fires of hell on a day when there has been a good intake of heretics. When it clears, a crystal brown caramel covers the surface of the pudding. Dona Amélia allows herself the luxury of an almost-smile. She has made *Leite-creme*, Burnt Cream, Portuguese caramel custard, one of the *pudims*, milk and egg puddings (often with a sauce) so common in Portugal that they call them the 365.

All nations express themselves through the food they eat, but few reveal their religion through their puddings. In contrast to main dishes, which are generally called something straightforward, Portuguese sweets often have names of child-like poetry: *Viuvinhas* – Little Widows; *Esquecidos* – Forgottens; *Ouriços* – Hedgehogs; *Pão Constipado* – Bread with a Cold in the Nose.

There is a playfulness and sense of fun here that contrasts with that other poetry, the *fado*, a desolate, keening song of nostalgia. But many other names of sweets are religious: *Celestes* – Heavenly Delights; *Emmanuels*. It was nuns who created *pudim*, because peasants lived in poverty. Treats were necessarily heaven-sent, like manna. The Portuguese reaction to the fancy food that came out of an institution vowed to poverty was neither bitterness nor resentment, but gentle irony, and a little fantasy. Irreverently, they ate – and eat – Nun's Tummies, Angel's Breasts, Nun's Nipples and Cardinal's Wet Nurse – recalling how an ailing dignitary was prescribed extra nourishment, in the days before vitamin pills. (In Amarante in the north there is even a harking-back to an older religion. In January and June the townspeople enjoy a fertility ritual in food – they bake brioche dough into phallic cakes and give them as presents to each other.)

So the tiny revelation I choose to find in Dona Amélia's caramel custard is of fun, poverty and tolerance. Portugal was a Catholic peasant society like Spain, but without the harshness: with exceptions – as in every nation – red-hot irons were for puddings, not for people.

# BURNT CREAM
## (*Leite-creme*)
### DONA AMÉLIA, LEÇA DA PALMEIRA, NEAR OPORTO
### ENOUGH FOR 4 TO 6 PEOPLE

| |
|---|
| **3 tablespoons plain flour** |
| **$\frac{1}{4}$ teaspoon nutmeg (optional)** |
| **250 ml (9 fl oz) water** |
| **2 tablespoons soft butter** |
| **A pinch of salt** |
| **1 or 2 strips of lemon peel** |
| **10 egg yolks** |
| **300 g (11 oz) sugar, and granulated sugar for the topping** |
| **A glass of port** |
| **1 litre (1$\frac{3}{4}$ pints) milk** |
| **And you'll need something very hot (see below)** |

PREPARATION: If you are using nutmeg, mix it with the flour. Stir in the water, then add the butter, salt and lemon peel, followed by the egg yolks, then the sugar, port and milk. Cook over a moderate heat – still stirring – until it thickens into a custard. Pour it into individual moulds.

When the little custards are quite cold, sprinkle the tops thickly with sugar, and caramelise them with something very hot. Work out how long to apply the heat by trial and error, starting at about 5 seconds.

〜 • 〜

A very hot grill is the usual way of caramelising the top, but such an easy solution not only goes against the True British Spirit of Improvisation: it chucks away the chance of exciting your guests with red-hot irons (which is much too good to miss).

Red-hot irons have had such a bad press ever since the Middle Ages that the average hardware store does not even stock anything to use on an insolent peasant, let alone on a pud. I have tried a blowlamp, but it puffs the sugar off. A thick old saucepan bottom might do. If you have a cleanish hunk of old metal around, you can hang it from wire to make a handle; but don't drop it on the carpet, or a guest.

Any of these solutions (or a professional salamander, which you can buy at shops for real chefs, at a price) is quite dangerous, which is always interesting.

~~ • ~~

We have a lot in common with the Portuguese: we share an ocean with them. They do not actually live on an island, like we do, but they have the next best thing – a corner, the westernmost point in Europe and a good jumping-off point for the rest of the world. There was a Portuguese queen of England and there was an English queen of Portugal – Catherine of Braganza and Philippa of Lancaster, respectively.

The Portuguese are seafarers, like the British: explorers, merchants, sailors of both our nations have been meeting each other in far-away places on and off the high seas for centuries. Portugal is ports abroad, and port at home: and the country itself is said to take its name from the town of Portus Cale, that once faced Oporto from the other side of the Douro gorge, near where the port wine lodges are now.

The wine that gives a slightly different taste to Dona Amélia's rather solid milk pud has made the British and the Portuguese more than old allies. They are drinking partners, bound together by every bottle of vintage, tawny and old crusted that has gone down the throats of English squires since 1703. Port was not originally a fortified wine: brandy was first added to help it withstand its voyage to Britain, where the customs asked only an eighth of what they charged on French wines. The squires liked the price and they liked the brandy; later, more fortification was added to suit the British taste.

Oporto citizens are traditionally known as tripe-eaters, from the days of their patriotic gesture to Prince Henry the Navigator, for whom they butchered their herds, victualling his ships so unselfishly that nothing was left for the townsfolk to eat but the tripes. Tripe remains a local speciality, cooked with smoked sausage and beans.

This is a city of cobbles, colour and energy: 'Coimbra sings, Braga prays, Lisbon plays, Oporto works', runs the proverb. People run, too; wine flows out; money rolls in. The Douro was named 'River of Gold' for the very best of reasons – it had nuggets in it – but there came to be more gold on the surface: barrels going downstream in flat-bottomed boats more like gondolas than barges. Transport by *rebelo* was developed in the last century by a Scotsman, Baron Forrester. The journey was not easy – there are rapids – and the inventor joined the exalted ranks of those, like M. Guillotin, who have paid their creations the ultimate homage. He drowned in one.

In Oporto harbour, the barrels were hoisted into British ships that smelt strongly of salt cod from the Newfoundland fishery. Without doubt, there were fishermen on the quay eating the same lunch as they do today – sardines fresh out of the sea grilled on charcoal. Smoke gets in your eyes, and the savour gets up your nose. For the best of *sardinhadas*, the fish must be small. People chew the flesh off sideways till only the skeleton is left. They call it 'playing the harmonica'. Otherwise, the fish are laid on slices of cornbread, which catch the juices. To make cornbread, replace half or two-thirds of the flour in your dough with polenta, and bake in the normal way: the result is rather coarse and cracks easily but tastes nuttier than ordinary bread. The other ritual accompaniment is roasted and peeled green peppers with olive oil dribbled over. Blacken the skins over a flame, and scrape off as much of the black as you feel inclined. Roasting softens the flesh and improves the flavour: few things taste better, and nothing on earth smells more savoury. (At home, if you prefer, you can do them under the grill or in the oven.)

With a salad of tomatoes that taste of the sun, not the cropability quotient, and naked ridge cucumbers – none of your floppy Dutch objects with a kinky plastic skin – such a meal is simple, but spiced with the greatest of all sauces – impermanence. It is cooked, it is eaten, it is gone; it is cooked tomorrow, it is different, it is a memory.

You cannot re-create such a meal when you are in one place in the world, and the very fresh local ingredients on which it relies are in another. Part of what you are cooking is an atmosphere, for which you have to go south; and for fish at the right stage of freshness, you must be near the water. The fish that put Portugal in the sandwiches of the world travels best in tins. Rather than an air-lifted sardine, I would choose a pilchard (very close in the same family) fresh out of the Cornish sea. Sprats are similar, too, and cheap. If your barbecue does not taste quite like Portugal, be glad that there are still some things far away; some things that still have seasons; some things that money cannot buy; and some few things that are better for poor people than for rich people.

Down the coast in the Estremadura, the Arrábida peninsula lies between two rivers – the Tagus and the estuary of the Sado. Sesimbra, an old fishing village of winding streets, is scarcely half an hour's drive from Lisbon, and prospers accordingly, with white terraces of verdant-balconied apartments and the sort of restaurants that lay you three glasses before you ask for them.

The fishermen are still there as well, however, spreading out the catch on the walls of the promenade, decorating their improvised counter with patterns of sand and stones. The *Manuel Chochinha*, bent in the middle like a banana, putters into harbour with gulls in its wake and a saucepan of remarkable size on deck, in which to make *caldeirada*, the Portuguese *bouillabaisse* that comes in not one but many varieties, according to the region and the catch. Markets sell bags of mixed fish; in the Algarve there is a *caldeirada* with lobster.

Sesimbra is famous for swordfish, but its firm white flesh is in demand for smoking and frying. The fishermen gut *pata-roxa*, a fish the colour of red mullet with a traily body and a blunt head; prepare frog-fish by stringing it up from its gaping mouth and peeling the skin from its body; fillet a ray; take thick conger eel and turn it into slices (cut from belly to head to avoid the bones). They begin the process of layering the fish in the pot with sliced onion, potatoes, tomatoes and parsley. Up on the hill in his elegant house, Duarte Leal, retired rugby footballer, has laid a Moorish-patterned table-cloth, retired to the kitchen, and is doing the same thing. (This is a good dish to have a rugby player make for you, since it seems to be a Portuguese principle never to make *Caldeirada Rica* in less than enormous quantities.)

The apparent simplicity of this dish hides some sophistication. The use of a layer of cockles to stop things burning on the bottom of the pan is ingenious; and it is important to think about how you cut things up and where you put them. The principle is the same as that of our own Bargee's Pail, in which an entire meal was cooked in a bucket, with everything arranged in layers, the food which needed the least cooking at the top. This is a dish made with what is available: dogfish, monkfish, huss, red and grey mullet, hake, cod, skate and haddock are among the names to consider in this country. Conger eel is very desirable. *Caldeirada* is often cooked in a fish stock made from the trimmings, but in this one most of the liquid comes out of the ingredients. Should you choose to add potatoes, put them near the bottom and cut them in slices so that they will be done without the fish being over-cooked. Fish cooks fast, but a big stew like this with little extra liquid takes longer. Even the shape of the party-size pot affects how long: but the *caldeirada* has its own clock. The slices of green peppers on top are there neither for flavour nor garnish. They are an indicator: when they are done, so is the *caldeirada*.

# FISH STEW
## (Caleirada Rica)
DUARTE LEAL, SESIMBRA

ENOUGH FOR 20 TO 30 PEOPLE

| |
|---|
| **8 kg (17 lb) (undressed weight) of 4 to 5 different kinds of fish, if possible including some conger eel** |
| **450 g (1 lb) cockles (or clams, or mussels)** |
| **6 fresh sardines** |
| **200 ml (7 fl oz) olive oil** |
| **2.5 kg (5½ lb) onions, sliced** |
| **4 kg (9 lb) tomatoes, sliced** |
| ***Piri-piri* sauce** |
| **Salt** |
| **200 ml (7 fl oz) port** |
| **2 green peppers, sliced** |

PREPARATION: Gut, skin, de-fin and otherwise prepare the fish, washing away the blood, and saving the livers. Remove bones according to your powers of endurance. (If you choose relatively boneless fish that hold together to start with, you can save either yourself or your guests a lot of work.) Cut into large chunks. Wash the cockles. Clean the sardines and cut off their heads.

Wet the bottom of the pan all over with olive oil and put in the cockles. Cover them with a layer of onion and a layer of tomatoes, sprinkling each layer with a few drops of *piri-piri*, salting it and wetting it with olive oil. Set aside the sardines, fish livers and peppers. Continue arranging everything else in layers, putting the more solid fish towards the bottom, with the same addition of *piri-piri*, salt and oil.

Pour the port over the top. Arrange the sardines and the fish livers in a star pattern, and strew with green pepper slices.

Cover the pan and cook the *caldeirada* over a moderate heat: it will be ready when the pepper slices are cooked. Discard the sardines before serving.

~ • ~

*Piri-piri* sauce, or something like it, is a flavouring no kitchen should be without. It is an essence of chilli — tabasco is one commercial alternative. *Piri-piri* itself comes from Mozambique, and is lemon juice which has had chillies, peppers and salt steeped in it. It is easy to make: cut up the chillies, mix everything, steep for a few days, and strain. Another version is like the chilli oil used in

Chinese cooking, and is made by throwing a handful of chillies, some lemon rind and a bay leaf into olive oil and standing the pot in the Portuguese sun. Given the English sun, warm the pot in a very slow oven for a few hours. (Break the skin of each chilli, to let the flavour escape.)

The British have a similar relic of their colonial days, sherry peppers, for which you simply cut up chillies and drown them in cheap sherry for a couple of weeks or so. Excellent for adding to soups, this is also the sort of flavouring you need to use drop by drop, though I prefer to moderate the heat and increase the flavour by using cut-up sweet red peppers to the extent of 2, 3 or 4 parts peppers to one of chillies. As the flavour becomes milder, the quality of the sherry (which should in any case be strong) becomes slightly more significant.

Lisbon owes both its architecture and its oysters to Britain, for its great – though sometimes ruthless – statesman, Pombal, lived in London in his youth. The oysters were imported in 1776; the Queen Anne style of the lower city had come following the Great Earthquake twenty-one years earlier, when the 'Sea of Straw', as the Tagus is called here because its waters are smooth and shiny, became a boiling tidal wave.

The first earthquake toppled the city like the wrath of God on All Saints' Day, when everybody was at Mass, with lighted candles in their hands; 250 convulsions followed during the next ten days; fires raged for five. Among the 17,000 buildings destroyed were 300 palaces and 110 churches. Freethinkers observed that God's timing of the event was unfortunate, and that, while the faithful in the churches had been gathered uncomfortably to their Maker, sinners in the prisons had survived rather well. It shocked the world then – though nowadays of course we know how to make much better disasters for ourselves. Today, Lisbon's equivalent of our Guy Fawkes is a penny for St Anthony in June, in memory of the charitable rebuilding of the churches.

Like its people, Lisbon is romantic, from its balconies of brilliant laundry to its Moorish-Gothic elevator by Eiffel. It is Olissibona, the legendary city of Ulysses; it was Roman, Moorish. Portuguese fishing boats often have eyes painted on the prow: they learned that from the Phoenicians. Even the public transport stirs the heart a little: the tram-cars up to the old town are like San Francisco's. Perhaps it is no more than you might expect of the capital of a country whose national day honours a poet (Luís de Camões), but Lisbon even succeeds in bringing a touch of romance to the codfish.

Salt cod is a staple of cooking in Lisbon and in Portugal generally: the sign of a Mediterranean Catholic culture, even though it just happens to be mostly on the Atlantic. All over Italy, Spain, France, the equivalent of *bacalhau* is a traditional Friday food for Catholics – easy to transport, easy to keep, cheap and plentiful. (Salt cod was once eaten in Britain more than it is now – a traditional English method was to flatten out the fillets, fry them in egg and breadcrumbs and serve with herb butter.) In Portugal they call it *fiel amigo*, faithful friend – and add that nowadays it is not as faithful as it used to be. They used to dine with their friend to the extent of a kilo a week for every man, woman and child, but *bacalhau* is dearer nowadays.

A fresh cod can weigh three-quarters of a hundredweight (36 kg). Salted and dried, it is tough stuff. Big white triangles of it hang at the doors of the grocers. Choose your piece, take it inside, and they cut it up with a guillotine. In Britain, West Indian grocers have it, and shops with Italian and Spanish foods, too. In Portugal on Fridays you can buy it ready soaked. Otherwise, any recipe begins with at least 24 hours' soaking with a couple of changes of water – they used to leave it in a fountain or a spring, so that the water changed itself.

*Bacalhau* is one up on the 365, the *pudim*: it has at least one variant for every day of a leap-year. They mash it with potatoes, put it in a tart, bake it in the oven with a cheese sauce, cook it in puréed onion; one dish accompanies it with turnips, cabbage, sprouts, onions, hard-boiled egg and potatoes – all doused with olive oil and crushed garlic. Possibly the most celebrated recipe is *Bacalhau à Bras*, a very unusual form of fish and chips. They did not think it beneath them in the posh restaurant where Horácio worked: chandeliers, ornate mirrors and wine warmed over a candle in a fancy-balconied terrace in a solid Lisbon street.

The kitchen was solid too – Portuguese kitchens are; not much in the way of gadgets apart from a wooden mandoline for fine-slicing vegetables and the biggest mouli in the world, made out of sheet metal, like they all used to be. The mandoline has not caught on in Britain. Useful as it is, its main role is as the thing that gets stuck in the kitchen drawer. The mouli has caught on, and jams up the kitchen drawer twice as effectively as the mandoline.

Horácio was a well-set-up young chef whose way with the toughness of salt cod was to treat it as if it had just flipped sand in his face with its tail. First – he cut the dry fish into strips, chopping through the bones with a heavy knife. Second – he fell upon the strips and tore the bones out of them with his bare hands. (It is also permissible to wait until after the soaking, when you can pick them out.) Third – he drowned the cod pieces for 24 hours. Fourth – he squeezed them until they were helpless. Fifth – having finally led the cod captive to the frying pan, he continued to demonstrate his contempt by tossing the entire contents into the air – cod, onions, oil and all – as if they were a mere pancake. (There is rhyme and reason to this, as it happens: after the soaking, cod becomes almost as soft as it was tough before – stirring it around over-vigorously breaks it up too much.) Sixth – he scrambled it. The codfish was thoroughly humiliated, and decided to live out the remainder of a rather short life in retirement on a silver platter, garnished – extremely respectably – with parsley.

# SALT COD À BRAS
## (Bacalhau à Bras)
HORÁCIO, LISBON

ENOUGH FOR 4 OR 5 PEOPLE

| |
|---|
| 600 g (1¼ lb) salt cod |
| Groundnut oil for deep-frying the chips |
| 1 kg (2¼ lb) potatoes, peeled and cut into fine chips |
| 2 onions, sliced |
| 3 cloves of garlic, chopped |
| Olive oil for frying the onions and garlic |
| 1 or 2 bay leaves |
| Pepper |
| 10 eggs, beaten |
| A few black olives |
| Parsley, chopped |

PREPARATION: Bone the cod and cut it into substantial pieces, removing any skin. Soak it until soft (24 hours in 2 changes of water). Heat the groundnut oil in a deep pan and start deep-frying the chips.

In another pan, soften the onions and garlic in olive oil with a bay leaf or two, until the onions are just golden. Take out the bay leaves. Gently but firmly, squeeze the water out of handfuls of salt cod. Add the cod to the onions and cook over moderate heat for about 10 minutes or so (cod gets sticky if it is overcooked). Season with pepper. Be careful how you handle the cod, but do not let it burn. Toss it, if you dare.

When the cod is cooked (try it and see), put most of the chips in with it and mix it all carefully (toss, if you like: second time lucky). Pour the beaten eggs over the cod and chips and fold everything together to mix. When the scrambling is complete, garnish with black olives, a border of the remaining chips and chopped parsley.

In Portugal they often drink red wine rather than white with both *bacalhau* and sardines.

Like another small nation that made a good thing out of exploiting the rest of the world, Portugal knows what it is to have tottering finances. It was a dictatorship for many years, and chaos before that; it became a democracy, but poor, with the lowest family income in Europe. But – rather more than the other small nation – it knows how to enjoy life, and how to value simple things, including a tradition of what we call 'peasant food'.

'Peasant food' is sometimes used as a term of dismissal. It is necessarily substantial (when the peasants can afford it), and is not necessarily beautiful. Some of the ingredients may make our pre-packed generation blench. But a peasant dish can contain within it balances of taste and texture no less felicitous than many posher creations. In Portugal, the qualities of peasant food have gone into the national cuisine. Even their table-settings are far more inclined to rusticity than to napery. A romantic simplicity suits the Portuguese, as it sometimes suits the British. They like the rose more than the rose bowl.

Take the simplest of soups, *Caldo Verde*, which originated in the northern province of the Minho. This is a green country which produces green wine, *vinho verde*, so it is only fitting that the soup should be green as well. It is made from nothing more than an onion, a potato and *couve galega*, a cabbage tall enough to be used as a minor hedge in cottage gardens, and from which people pluck the leaves as they need them. This soup is made everywhere in Portugal, though in the south they tend to serve it in a plate where the north brings it in a cup. It is eaten with cornbread, a spoon of good olive oil and a slice of *chouriço*, a hard meat sausage with red pepper and garlic. (*Chouriço* is similar to the Spanish *chorizo*, which is fairly easily obtainable in this country.)

*Caldo Verde* is very cheap and very easy, but it needs quality and care. Use a potato that tastes like one, and be obsessive in your slicing of the greens. (*Couve galega* is not to be found in Britain, so use whatever greens are available; you can ring the changes by shredding Swiss chard, spinach or even cos lettuce.) The cutting is really extremely fine: a counsel of reasonable perfection is to start at 1 mm ($\frac{1}{16}$ inch) and work downwards. You should end up with what the French call a *chiffonade*. Then the cabbage cooks *al dente* in the short space of time between being put into the hot soup and arriving at table. I find this plainest of plain dishes a revelation in the balance of simple flavours. Portuguese food could have no better ambassador than *Caldo Verde*, which I translate as 'hot green stuff' – though it begins with the cold white stuff.

# POTATO AND CABBAGE SOUP
## (Caldo Verde)
HORÁCIO, LISBON

ENOUGH FOR 4 PEOPLE

| |
|---|
| 700 g (1½ lb) potatoes, peeled |
| 1 large onion, peeled and cut into quarters |
| 1½ litres (2½ pints) water |
| About 7 tablespoons olive oil |
| Salt |
| 150 g (5 oz) cabbage, finely shredded |
| 4 slices of *chouriço* |
| 4 slices of cornbread |

PREPARATION: Put the potatoes and onion in a large pan with the water and add 2 tablespoons of olive oil and some salt. Bring to the boil and boil for 15 to 20 minutes, until the vegetables are done. Mash the vegetables or purée them through a mouli into the same water. Bring back to the boil and throw in the shredded cabbage with 2 more tablespoons of olive oil. Boil for a few seconds while you toss the sausage slices in a little oil in a frying pan. Pour the soup into bowls and dribble half a tablespoon of olive oil on top of each. Serve accompanied by the sausage and cornbread.

Towards the south of the country is a large province full of that not-quite-emptiness peculiar to plainlands which are devoting all their energies to growing grain. The Alentejo shivers in winter and bakes in summer, but it has given *açorda* to the nation.

*Açorda* is another kind of soup, and the product of another very simple principle – when your bread gets stale, you moisten it with something tasty. There is not much incentive to make a soup out of sliced bread, which is always soft and tasted of very little in the first place. But I have found, when camping in the Midi, that the accumulation of crusts going stale so quickly in the heat almost compels one towards a dish like this; and I tasted bread soup before I ever knew there was such a thing as a *panada*.

*Panada* is a name for any kind of bread- or crumb-bound mix. The stuffing you put in a chicken is a *panada*. Bread soup is a *panada* too, and *panada* is what I prefer to call it, since 'bread soup' sounds so off-putting.

Soup was to the countrymen of the Alentejo what bread and cheese was to the British farm labourer. It was carried off to work in the wheat-fields or with the sheep in a *tarro*, a small cork bucket which helped keep a *gazpacho* cold in summer or an *açorda* warm in winter. Many things were luxuries in inland Portugal, away from the cosmopolitan cities of the coast, and *açorda* was often very simple, flavoured only with olive oil, garlic and herbs (pennyroyal or coriander, perhaps), with an egg for nourishment. *Açorda* is all over Portugal now, however, and this one, which Dona Amélia made in Oporto, is quite grand. A strong chicken stock gives it lots of background flavour, with shrimps for luxury — and a Portuguese quantity of eggs.

# SHRIMP PANADA
## (*Açorda de Camarão*)
### DONA AMÉLIA, LEÇA DA PALMEIRA, NEAR OPORTO
### ENOUGH FOR 4 TO 6 PEOPLE

| |
|---|
| $\frac{1}{2}$ chicken, jointed |
| 1 large onion, sliced |
| About 1·5 litres ($2\frac{1}{2}$ pints) water |
| 4 tablespoons butter or margarine (Dona Amélia used margarine) |
| Salt and pepper |
| 200 ml (7 fl oz) white wine |
| 1 kg ($2\frac{1}{4}$ lb) cooked shrimps |
| 300 g (11 oz) stale bread (e.g. 6 rolls a couple of days old) |
| 6 eggs |
| *Piri-piri* sauce (see p. 94) |

PREPARATION: Put the chicken and the onion in a large pan with the water. Add the butter and season with salt and pepper. Simmer, covered, for about $1\frac{1}{2}$ hours, to make a broth. Add the wine 10 minutes before the end.

Put a few shrimps aside for a garnish and peel the rest. Tear the bread into pieces and simmer it in lightly salted water for a few minutes, until it is soft. Drain it, pressing it a little with a spoon. Put it in a saucepan. Strain the broth and add enough of it to the bread to make a very sloppy mixture. Stir it well over a medium heat. (The broth will be buttery and should be quite strong.)

Let it continue cooking while you separate 3 eggs and beat the yolks with 3 more whole eggs. Stir these vigorously into the *panada*, add the shrimps and season with *piri-piri*. The completed dish is substantial but tasty, and of a similar texture to very sloppy scrambled eggs.

The Alentejo has flocks of sheep on the plains and black pigs eating acorns in the groves of cork oaks, red-trunked where the cork has been stripped. The acorns are said to give the pork a particularly good flavour, and the white truffles the pigs sometimes root up to impart a very special quality indeed. Personally I would rather taste my truffles by a less roundabout route, or at least be assured that my particular pork chop had had its proper share of fungi. But for the famous dish of the region – Pork Loin with Cockles – I would forgo the guarantee: partly because it is such a good dish in itself, and partly because it is such a powerful affair that a hint of anything would go unnoticed.

The recipe begins three months before serving, with the laying down of sweet red (or possibly green) peppers in coarse salt, to be washed and minced nearer the time. If you want to serve Alentejo Pork Loin with Cockles three months early, you can make a sweet pepper paste by liquidising fresh or preserved peppers with salt, and perhaps a little onion and chilli.

When preparing shellfish, always discard any light or open shells, and shells which refuse to open when cooked. Cockles have an impressive ability to collect sand, and getting rid of it may require a lot of washing – it can take several changes of water with the cockles left for an hour in each, and then overnight soaking in salted water. But with luck it may be enough to salt a large pan of water, thoroughly mix in a cup of flour and leave the cockles in that for 12 hours. The theory is that in eating the flour they get rid of more sand, and flour is cheap enough to give this method the benefit of the doubt. If you use mussels, scrub them and scrape off the beards coming out of the shells, then wash them in two changes of water, leaving them at least an hour in the first.

# PORK LOIN WITH COCKLES

## A WOMAN OF ÉVORA, ALTA ALENTEJO
### ENOUGH FOR 10 TO 12 PEOPLE

| |
|---|
| 2¼ kg (5 lb) pork loin |
| 3 cloves of garlic |
| 3 tablespoons coarse salt |
| 200 ml (7 fl oz) sweet pepper paste |
| 3 kg (6½ lb) cockles, clams or mussels |
| 250 g (9 oz) lard for frying |
| 450 g (1 lb) bread, sliced |
| 125 ml (4 fl oz) white wine |
| *Garnish* |
| Lemon slices |
| Slices of radish |

PREPARATION: Take any fat off the meat and from the lighter-coloured end cut six 5 cm (2 inch) slices almost all the way through. Chop the rest of the meat into separate slices of the same thickness, and cut each one across once to make two chunks. Pound the garlic with the salt and rub it well all over the meat. Cover the meat with sweet pepper paste and leave it in a cool place for 24 hours.

Prepare the shellfish as necessary. Put a kettle on to boil.

Fry the meat chunks in lard and put them into a large pan to keep warm. Cut the slices down the middle to make steaks about 2 cm (¾ inch) thick and fry them, keeping them warm separately when they are done. Fry slices of bread rapidly in the fat and set them aside. Pour the remaining fat over the meat chunks.

Heat a large empty saucepan and throw in the cockles. Pour boiling water from the kettle over them, and shake the pan to encourage them to open. When they are open, wet them with the white wine and cook until boiling, shaking the pan vigorously.

Combine the cockles and their juices in one saucepan with the meat chunks, turning everything over to mix it. Pour the contents of this saucepan into a heated serving dish, arrange the meat slices and the slices of fried bread around the sides, and garnish with slices of lemon and radish.

Hungary: Gundel Pancakes page 107

# LANDS OF FIRE

## HUNGARY AND PAKISTAN

### HUNGARY

*'Let the fogs not stifle, the hail bruise, the storm break, nor fire destroy the only hope of our poor country.'* The blessing of the wheatfields on St Mark's day, 25 April

Hungary and Pakistan are two sides of the same nomadic free-for-all between East and West. Both countries have been much invaded, and they have invaders in common. But the principal invaders of Hungary were seven tribes who arrived towards the end of the ninth century AD, with flights of arrows, flurries of hooves and the customary brutalities.

The Magyars were the leaders among the seven tribes; and the name has come to embody a fire and bravado which have never quite disappeared through all the adulterating centuries in which the warrior race who had settled down, most of them, found themselves a target for other warrior races who hadn't. A fiercely independent people spent a lot of their history not being independent at all. There was a brief but total devastation by the Mongols in the mid-thirteenth century, and in the sixteenth and seventeenth centuries there was a long period of Turkish rule over most of the country. Then in 1699 Hungary became subject to the Austrian Empire.

Pakistan: Spicy Vegetable Fritters page 130

The young horsemen who felt the fighting spirit of the Magyars running in their veins went off and became hussars in other armies. The rest of the Hungarians got on with being peasants, aristocrats, bourgeois, according to their luck – and, occasionally, patriots. So Hungary as a rather nonconformist chip on the Communist bloc with a heroic but unsuccessful resistance in its recent past is Hungary as it has often been before.

# BUDAPEST AND THE NORTH-EAST

*'The Slovaks all drink brandy,*
*The Germans all drink beer.*
*Hungarians – nothing else but wine,*
*And that the best, my dear . . .'*
Traditional song

Three turbulent centuries in the Middle Ages and fifty years of relative independence before the 1914–18 war were Hungary's times of independent creativity. The first period ended with the reign of Matthias the Just, whose wife was Beatrice of Naples; the second included a lesser dynasty – the Gundels. Both had important consequences for Hungarian cooking.

No better can be said of a king than that he cared for his subjects in peace, won his wars, built a library, and encouraged his cooks, and in all of these Matthias was a paragon. After his reign more than his conquests was lost: the people said, 'The king is dead, and justice with him.' Nor did the library go unscathed when the Turks entered Budapest in 1541. But the figs, turkeys, onions and garlic that he and Beatrice introduced from Italy have never ceased to gladden Hungarian stomachs.

The taste for sophisticated cooking begun during this renaissance developed further with the importation of French chefs by Hungarian aristocrats, and then at the court of Vienna, to which the nobility gravitated during the long years of Hapsburg domination. When Hungary achieved a reasonable equality with Austria during the second half of the nineteenth century, there was a flowering of innovation in food fashion, headed by the Gundel dynasty of restaurateurs, by János Gundel and his son Károly.

Gundel pancakes are one of the family recipes in great demand in Hungary's best restaurants. They are so rich and alcoholic that when I first saw the recipe I could not understand how someone with the discrimination of a Gundel could flambé them as well, as is the custom nowadays – often with the assistance of a gipsy band going full scrape. But I have the opinion of George Lang, author of the outstanding *The Cuisine of Hungary*, to the effect that Károly himself never did. The thing to watch is that pancakes, filling and sauce are hot when you serve them. If necessary, you can reheat the pancakes in a buttered frying pan. The filling can get a bit heavy and dry, but if you chop some of the walnuts rather than grinding them, and moisten with extra rum and some cream, you will avoid stodginess. Half the milk can be replaced with fizzy water, added just before cooking.

# GUNDEL PANCAKES
## (*Gundel Palacsinta*)
GYULA GULLNER, DUNA INTERCONTINENTAL HOTEL, BUDAPEST
ENOUGH FOR 4 TO 6 PEOPLE

| |
|---|
| 125 g (4½ oz) flour |
| Salt |
| 2 eggs |
| 250 ml (9 fl oz) milk |
| 2 teaspoons sugar |
| 25 g (1 oz) butter, softened or melted |
| *Filling* |
| 25 g (1 oz) sultanas |
| A glass of rum |
| 125 ml (4 fl oz) milk |
| 100 g (4 oz) walnuts, ground or chopped |
| 100 g (4 oz) sugar |
| Grated rind of ½ lemon |
| *Chocolate sauce* |
| 125 ml (4 fl oz) double cream |
| 250 ml (9 fl oz) milk |
| ¼ of a vanilla pod or a few drops of vanilla essence |
| 75 g (3 oz) plain chocolate, broken into small pieces |
| 50 g (2 oz) cocoa powder |
| 2 egg yolks |
| 125 g (4½ oz) sugar |
| 2 glasses of rum |

PREPARATION: Put the sultanas for the filling to soak in the rum.

Make the pancakes. Sieve the flour, with a pinch of salt, into a bowl. Whisk in the eggs, the milk, the sugar and the butter. If you have time, leave the batter to rest for an hour or two. Heat a very little butter or oil in a heavy pan. Pour in just enough batter to cover the base of the pan and swirl it round. When the top of the pancake begins to look dry and lacy and the edges curl – this takes about half a minute – turn it over and cook the other side. Slide the pancake on to a warmed dish. Repeat the process with the rest of the batter.

To make the filling, bring the milk to the boil and add the walnuts, the sugar, the grated lemon rind and the soaked sultanas, with any rum they haven't absorbed. Simmer to reduce the mixture to a moist paste. If the filling gets dry, add a little cream.

For the sauce, put the cream, milk, vanilla, chocolate and cocoa powder in a saucepan over a low heat. Cook very gently until the chocolate melts. Off the heat, whisk in the egg yolks, the sugar and the rum. Return the pan to a low heat and cook, stirring all the time, until the sauce thickens. Be very careful not to let it boil.

Put about a tablespoon of filling on each pancake and fold it in four. Arrange the pancakes on a hot dish and pour the sauce over them. Flambé, if you like.

With its pastry and coffee shops, its inns and taverns, Hungary has a long tradition of public eating and drinking – of open enjoyment. The Gundels' achievement was not only a matter of setting up a high-class restaurant (that can be done in most places, and often expires with the retirement of the cook) but to bring into its good taste the flavour of the people's cooking. *Palócleves* is an example of this. It is a version of the traditional *gulyás*, but it is far from authentic, since it contains forbidden ingredients – cream and flour (Gyula Gullner adds wine as well). Having become popular, the recipe has acquired variations, but the essential theme is diced lamb with green beans. The fat used for the frying would traditionally have been lard, as it was in most Hungarian stews. The crucial thing is to add each of the main vegetables at the right stage, so that none of them overcooks. Some writers advise cooking them separately.

# PALÓCS SOUP
## (*Palócleves*)
GYULA GULLNER, DUNA INTERCONTINENTAL HOTEL, BUDAPEST

ENOUGH FOR 4 PEOPLE

| |
|---|
| 1 onion, finely chopped |
| Oil for frying |
| 1 heaped teaspoon paprika |
| 300 g (11 oz) lean lamb, cut into 1 cm ($\frac{1}{2}$ inch) dice and washed |
| 1 teaspoon caraway |
| 1 bay leaf |
| About 2 teaspoons salt |
| Pepper |
| 1 clove of garlic, very finely chopped |
| 2 carrots, cut into 5 mm ($\frac{1}{4}$ inch) dice |
| 1 stick of celery, halved |
| About 1 litre ($1\frac{3}{4}$ pints) water |
| 1 potato, diced |
| 1 sweet pepper, diced |
| 100 g (4 oz) green beans, chopped into 1 cm ($\frac{1}{2}$ inch) lengths |
| Dry white wine or lemon juice (optional) |
| 50 g (2 oz) flour |
| 250 ml (9 fl oz) soured cream |
| 1 tomato, diced |
| *Garnish* |
| Chives, chopped |

PREPARATION: In a saucepan, fry the onion briskly in the oil until it begins to soften. Stir in paprika, the meat, caraway, bay leaf, and a rough seasoning of salt and pepper. Fry for 3 or 4 minutes, stirring as necessary and making sure that the paprika does not burn. Add the garlic, carrot and celery and pour in water to cover (about 750 ml/$1\frac{1}{4}$ pts). Simmer, uncovered, for about half an hour, topping up the water as needed. Now add the potato. After another 10 minutes put in the sweet pepper, and 5 minutes later the green beans. If you like, add a little dry white wine or lemon juice. Add water as necessary.

Five minutes before the end of cooking add the tomato to the stew, stir in the cream thickened with the flour and a little water. Simmer till the beans are done. Take out the celery and garnish with chopped chives.

The Palócs are people of the north-eastern hills directly descended from tribes who accompanied the original Magyars, and the soup was created at the request of their most distinguished writer, Kálmán Mikszáth, who was known as 'the Great Palóc'. A colourful people, they make what has to be the most alcoholic wedding cake in the world – a plait of dough with a hole in the middle for a bottle of honeyed brandy to encourage the happy couple on their wedding night. Another tradition of the Hungarian wedding is the 'Dance of the Cooks', performed by all those who prepared the wedding feast, carrying kitchen utensils in their hands. The Palócs are known for their folk art, as are the Matyó, who live between the hills and the Great Plain and embroider costumes as flowery as a runaway lawnmower in a herbaceous border.

The Matyó dish Chicken in Broth is a soup pretty enough to grace any wedding. The cooking times are rather dependent on the bird. If it is old, it needs to cook longer on its own (say, three-quarters of an hour) before you add the vegetables. But the process is poaching, not stewing out all the goodness, so for an average bird the time needed is comparatively short.

# CHICKEN IN BROTH WITH FRESH TARRAGON
## (*Matyós Tyuk*)
### GYULA GULLNER, IN MEZÖKÖVESD
ENOUGH FOR 4 PEOPLE

| |
|---|
| 1·5 litres (2½ pints) water |
| 1 youngish chicken |
| 1 onion |
| 1 stick of celery |
| Salt and white pepper |
| 3 carrots, cut into strips |
| 1 small parsnip, cut into strips |
| ½ head of cauliflower, divided into sprigs |
| 50 g (2 oz) mushrooms, sliced |
| 50 g (2 oz) butter |
| 50 g (2 oz) flour |
| A handful of parsley, chopped |
| 6 branches of fresh tarragon, chopped |
| 125 ml (4 fl oz) soured cream |
| 2 egg yolks |

PREPARATION: Put the water on to boil, in a large pan. Cut the chicken into small pieces and wash them: giblets and all can go in for the benefit of the broth, but only the meat is served. Put the meat in the boiling water, skimming well when it returns to the boil. Add the onion and celery whole, salt approximately and turn the heat down to a low simmer. Cook for about 5 minutes (but see note above).

Strew the carrots, parsnip, cauliflower and mushrooms on top of the chicken. Simmer for a further 30 minutes, or until the chicken is done.

Meanwhile, prepare a thickening. Melt the butter, add the flour and cook for 3 to 4 minutes. Add the chopped parsley and dilute the mixture with cold water. Take the onion, celery and chicken giblets out of the soup and stir in the thickening, then the tarragon. Bring the soup to the boil while you beat the cream with the egg yolks in a bowl. Take the soup off the heat and stir in the cream and egg liaison. Do not let the soup boil again.

Hungary's most famous and most advertised wines come from slopes of the north: 'the king of wine, and the wine of kings' from the twenty-five Tokay villages, and Bikavér, Bull's Blood, from Eger in the Bükk Hills (though a particularly celebrated Bikavér also comes from Szekszárd in the south; and other wine areas include Lake Balaton, where the most distinguished Badacsony wine has the unusual name of Kéknyelü (Blue-handled), with two sub-categories, 'Long-handled' and 'Short-handled'. The quality of Tokay – tangy, golden and sweet – is measured in bucketfuls, *puttonyos*, of the shrivelled grapes that give the wine its special flavour; 3, 4 or 5 are the usual grades, with 6 a rarity: and Tokay Essencia is made entirely from the juice of the *aszú*, as the grapes of concentrated sweetness are called.

There are many stories about the origin of the name Bull's Blood, most of them contemptuous of the Turks, who are said to have fled before the men of Eger whose beards were stained with wine – thinking that the Hungarians had been drinking blood – or to have used the name as an excuse to break their Muslim vow of temperance. Eger is honeycombed with secret passages dug into the soft volcanic rock at the time of the Turkish occupation (nowadays they make excellent wine-cellars). Its fortress garrison of 2000 men, women and children is said to have accounted for 40,000 Turks during a six-week siege; but in due course the city fell.

The Bükk Hills behind Eger take their name from the birch trees which grow there along with the mixed forests of fir and beech that provided fuel for potash, limestone and charcoal-burning. Near the bosky Szalajka valley with its trout stream and waterfalls is Szilivásvárad, where the Counts of Pallavicini once lived in a solid mansion that is now a trade union holiday hotel. The horses of the Lipica stud run in the fields, and the equestrian centre nearby is the home of the world-beating Hungarian riders – notably their champion four-in-hand team. Gyula Gullner made Horseman's Special for the Olympic gold-medallist György Bárdos and his friends at a restaurant in Eger.

The Special – marinated steak rolled round a filling and stewed in a sauce – is a good dish for an occasion. It is one of the many variations upon the *rostélyos*, a steak dish which is often the result of improvisation. Sirloin steak is particularly suitable for this sort of dish. The steak needs to be thick enough to slice through and open out. A thinner steak can be cut through horizontally, leaving a good hinge of meat along one edge; a thicker, more compact one can be sliced down through the middle (leaving a hinge) and then each half sliced horizontally from the middle out (leaving hinges). How long you can marinate the steak depends on the steak and on the weather, but the longer the soak, the more easily it will hammer out to a large, thin sheet.

Ordinary mushrooms with some dried *porcini* from an Italian delicatessen can be substituted for forest mushrooms such as ceps and chanterelles. The bacon should be green or only lightly smoked. The combination of fresh peppers cooked with good sweet tomatoes and onions is *lecsó* – one of the basic mixes of Hungarian cookery, and one of the great tastes of the world.

# HORSEMAN'S SPECIAL
## (*Csikós Kedvence*)
### GYULA GULLNER, IN EGER
### ENOUGH FOR 4 PEOPLE

| |
|---|
| 2 sirloin steaks, each weighing about 300 g (11 oz) |
| 200 ml (7 fl oz) oil |
| 1 tablespoon French mustard |
| Salt and pepper |
| 200 g (7 oz) chanterelles or ceps, or 150 g (5 oz) ordinary mushrooms and some dried *porcini* |
| Oil for frying |
| 1 onion, chopped |
| 1 sweet pepper chopped |
| 1 tomato, chopped |
| 4 rashers of smoked streaky bacon, chopped |
| About 200 ml (7 fl oz) dry white wine |
| About 1 tablespoon paprika |

| *Stuffing* |
| --- |
| 2 rashers of smoked streaky bacon, chopped into 6 mm ($\frac{1}{4}$ inch) strips |
| Oil for frying |
| 1 onion, thinly sliced |
| 1 sweet pepper, chopped |
| 1 tomato, chopped |
| 1 bunch of parsley, chopped |
| 125 g ($4\frac{1}{2}$ oz) cooked rice |
| 50 g (2 oz) chicken livers, chopped |
| 100 g (4 oz) pork, minced |
| 1 egg |
| Salt and pepper |
| *Garnish* (optional) |
| 2 tomatoes, sliced |
| Parsley, chopped |

PREPARATION: Marinate the steaks with 200 ml (7 fl oz) oil, the mustard and some pepper in a cool place for at least 2 days. If you are using dried mushrooms, put them to soak in a little warm water.

Make the stuffing. Fry the bacon lightly in oil over a moderate heat. Add the onion. When the onion is golden brown, take the pan off the heat and mix in all the rest of the stuffing ingredients thoroughly. Season with salt and pepper.

Slice each steak almost through and open it out (see above). Hammer it thin. Put the filling on the centre of the meat, fold in the sides, roll it up into a fat sausage shape and tie it with string. Season the steak parcels with salt and pepper and sear them in hot oil over a high heat. Lower the heat and add the onion, pepper, tomato and bacon to the meat. Pour on half the white wine and water just to cover. Simmer without a lid for about 50 minutes or until the meat is tender.

About 15 minutes before the end of cooking, drain dried mushrooms, or wipe fresh ones and chop. The liquid in the pan will be reduced by about half. Add the remaining wine, the mushrooms and the paprika. Adjust the seasoning. When the mushrooms are done (in 5 to 10 minutes), take the string off the steak rolls and slice them diagonally. Place the slices on a serving dish, pour the sauce over and garnish, if you like, with tomato slices and chopped parsley.

Gyula Gullner served the Special with roast potatoes, fried cabbage and tomato shells filled with florets of broccoli, buttered and baked in the oven. It was followed by Hungarian dumplings. Hungarians are good with flour in many ways, from breads via the decorated honey cakes and gingerbreads which for generations have delighted children at the fair to cakes quite as wicked as anything in Vienna.

Among Hungarian dumplings of various flours – *galuskas*, 'morsels' of egg dough, dumplings sweet, savoury, fruit or meat – is the are *gombóc*, often enriched with some kind of cheese or cream. This recipe has both, as well as fresh farm-tasting Hungarian butter, and is a little fancy with its separate whipping of the egg whites. Do not rest the dough, and do not overwork it.

# COTTAGE CHEESE DUMPLINGS
## (*Túrós Gombóc*)
### GYULA GULLNER, IN EGER
### ENOUGH FOR 4 PEOPLE

| |
|---|
| 40 g (1½ oz) butter |
| 225 g (8 oz) cottage cheese or curd cheese |
| 100 g (4 oz) flour (preferably strong flour) |
| Salt |
| 3 eggs, separated |
| 100 g (4 oz) breadcrumbs |
| Butter (with a little oil) for frying |
| 125 ml (4 fl oz) soured cream |

PREPARATION: Heat a pan of salted water to simmering point. Cream the butter with the cottage cheese, the flour, a little salt and the egg yolks. Beat the egg whites until stiff, and mix the cheese mixture into them. Form the dumplings by taking out small spoonfuls of dough, using a wet spoon so that they slip off it easily. Pop them in the simmering water. When they float to the top, they should be done.

Fry the breadcrumbs in a mixture of butter and oil until they are golden brown. Toss the dumplings in the pan until they are well coated with crumbs. Pour soured cream over them and serve.

# THE GREAT PLAIN

*'Here is the world's centre!*
*(If you doubt it, enter.)'*
Rhyme traditionally posted over the doors of Hungarian taverns

Hungary is warm-hearted: most of the country has thermal water underground, often near enough to the surface to be used for central heating and warming greenhouses. It is also warm-stomached – but not as warm as all that, because paprika, the Hungarian spice, is not chilli powder.

Originally from South America, where cooks draw fine distinctions between a bewildering number of varieties, sweet and chilli peppers made their way gradually east from Spain, arriving in Hungary at the time of the Turks. Paprika was originally known as 'Turkish pepper'. For at least 250 years paprika was made from dried peppers which were trodden like wine-grapes, then laboriously ground into a spice which was exceedingly fiery, and condemned by the aristocracy as fit only for peasants. Selective milling of flesh and seeds (in which the fire is concentrated) began in the middle of the nineteenth century, enabling a range of paprikas to be produced, from mild to inflammatory. The hottest is *erős* paprika: the next, and most-used, is *rózsa*: and via such categories as *féledes* (semi-sweet), *édesnemes* (sweet-noble, with the beginnings of a bite), paprikas descend to *csemegepaprika, csípősségmentes* paprika, and – the King of the milder qualities – *különleges* paprika: fine-ground and spicy. In Britain you will be lucky to find a shop which can offer you even two of the half-dozen varieties common in Hungary. I conducted a tasting of all the varieties I could find in London. The prices varied by several hundred per cent, but with the exception of the most expensive, which was rather sweeter and more aromatic, there was little to choose between them. Paprika does not keep very well, so use the freshest possible.

Probably because of its colour, paprika retains a certain romance, even in lands far away from the fields that in harvest-time are aflame with red and yellow, and the houses where they hang garlands of brilliant fruit to dry from the eaves. It is like buying the sun, or a lick of Hungarian fire.

It was just what the peasant had been seeking for the stew which he and his ancestors had been making in much the same way for many centuries. Stew – or, in its more liquid form, soup – is part of Hungarian history, not only a peasant staple but an early convenience food: for in time of war or travel they would boil it down to the chunks, and carry the dehydrated bits off in their saddlebags. *Gulyás*, from which we have made 'goulash' (which would often be better described as 'ghoulash'), originally means a herdsman. There are still herdsmen on the Great Plain, ranging from whip-cracking cowboys to shepherds as patient among their flocks as the waiting dogs.

It is unreasonable that anything should be as flat as the landscape of Hortobágy, south-east of the Matyóföld. The *puszta* is a lawn under a sky: the emptiness is not only a monument to nature - the villages became ghost towns when the Turks came. The southern plains have become a garden, but the stop in their process of development caught the *puszta* in its change from swamp to pasture like a hiccup in history, and preserved something of a way of life that is very old indeed. On these pastures a hierarchy of herdsmen – from horse-breeders to swineherds – led a scattered and lonely existence with the most primitive shelter. Shepherds almost carried their houses on their backs, in the shape of an enormous tent-like cloak of sheepskin, in which the wearer would sit totally enclosed but for his head, like the occupant of a patent individual Turkish bath. A good plains cook asked no more than a pot, a fire and something to keep the wind off.

It is difficult to find a focus for an empty space on which most things – sheep, people and horses – are always moving about: and the best bet is the Nine-hole Bridge straddling the river at Hortobágy, its long white arches echoed in the colonnades of the Nagycsárda, the Great Inn, which has an equally great history of acquaintance with highwaymen, for the *puszta* was a natural refuge for outlaws. At the inn they serve *gulyás* in metal bowls with handles that resemble the plainsmen's cauldron.

Gyula Gullner's lamb *gulyás* can also be made with beef – and more likely would be in other parts of Hungary. It can also be made with a less extravagant cut of lamb, but it will then need longer cooking. It is a straightforward dish. *Gulyás* ceases to be *gulyás* if it is much elaborated: if you want to add another spice, it should be caraway seed. Be careful not to burn the paprika at the start, and watch the quantity of liquid (for a *gulyás* is never thickened with flour). There should be enough to swim round the meat and potatoes, but not enough to drown them. To start with, assume that you need very little more liquid than what is in the vegetables, plus the water on the meat when it comes out of the wash (which is one of the reasons for following Mr Gullner's enthusiasm for washing it).

If you can find sweet peppers with real flavour, it will make a worthwhile difference. The answer to the question 'How hot is a hot pepper?' is whatever you can get that suits your taste, but be careful of Indian chillies. The Hungarian chilli is called 'cherry paprika', but there is a vast range of different heats of peppers in the world, often varying from district to district in the same country, and even the most complex system, the Mexican, makes no real sense internationally. Use your judgement, see the note on how to tame chillies in the following section on Pakistan (page 122), and, if you make a mistake, comfort your burning tastebuds with the thought that the Hungarians used to sprinkle hot paprika on wounds as an antiseptic.

# LAMB GOULASH
## (Bárány Gulyás)
GYULA GULLNER, ON THE PUSZTA
ENOUGH FOR 4 TO 6 PEOPLE

| |
|---|
| 2 good-sized onions, very finely chopped |
| Lard or oil for frying |
| 2 sweet peppers, 1 diced, 1 cut into strips |
| 2 tomatoes, 1 diced, 1 sliced |
| 1 clove of garlic, very finely chopped |
| 5 heaped teaspoons *rózsa* or standard paprika |
| 1 kg ($2\frac{1}{4}$ lb) leg of lamb, cubed and washed in cold water |
| About 2 teaspoons salt |
| About $\frac{1}{2}$ teaspoon hot paprika |
| 1 stick of celery, halved |
| 4 potatoes, cubed |
| 1 hot pepper, cut into strips |

PREPARATION: Sizzle the onions in the fat with the diced sweet peppers and tomatoes until the onion is golden, adding the garlic towards the end. Mix in the paprika, and after a few seconds moisten with a very little water to prevent the spice burning. Add the meat cubes straight from the water in which they have been washed. Season with salt and a little hot paprika and add the stick of celery. Stir well and cook uncovered over moderate heat for about 30 to 40 minutes – or until you judge that the meat is 15 minutes from being done. This will depend on the cut, but you should aim to have the meat just tender rather than very soft. Stir as necessary and add water if you need to (at the end there should be not quite enough liquid to cover).

Add the potatoes, the pepper strips and the slices of tomato. Correct the seasoning, and cook for another 15 minutes or so, until the vegetables are done. Serve the *gulyás* with bread or dumplings.

I have described a dryish version of *gulyás*, which is the most liquid of the stews traditional in Hungary. *Pörkölt* is the opposite of the *gulyás*, using similar sorts of ingredients but cooking them covered, without extra water. Then, *paprikás* is like *pörkölt*, but with cream: and the meat in *tokány* is in ribbons rather than chunks and its other ingredients are likely to include smoked bacon. This *tokány* is in the style of Debrecen, the town to the east of the Great Plain, which is famous for its sausages. Substitute a Spanish *chorizo*-style sausage or a thin salami rather than a British banger. The dish is highly spiced for a *tokány*, for the 'hot pepper' was actually a whole cherry paprika; but the real change in character between this and the goulash is the addition of cream.

# HORSEMAN'S STEW
## (Csikós Tokány)
GYULA GULLNER, ON THE *PUSZTA*
ENOUGH FOR 4 TO 6 PEOPLE

| |
|---|
| 150 g (5 oz) smoked streaky bacon, chopped into 6 mm ($\frac{1}{4}$ inch) strips |
| Lard or oil for frying |
| 2 onions, sliced |
| 2 sweet peppers, chopped |
| 2 tomatoes, chopped |
| 2 teaspoons paprika |
| 800 g (1$\frac{3}{4}$ lb) good-quality braising steak, trimmed, cut across the grain into ribbons about 6 mm ($\frac{1}{4}$ inch) wide and 7 cm (3 inches) long, and washed |
| About 2 teaspoons salt |
| Pepper |
| 1 chilli, broken into pieces |
| 150 ml ($\frac{1}{4}$ pint) soured cream and a little (optional) extra for garnish |
| 25 g (1 oz) flour |
| 200 g (7 oz) smoked sausage, sliced |
| *Garnish* (optional) |
| Tomato slices |
| Sweet pepper slices |
| Parsley, chopped |

PREPARATION: Fry the bacon lightly in the lard or oil in a large pan. Add the onions and fry fairly briskly until they are getting golden, then add the peppers and tomatoes. Continue cooking, uncovered, until the peppers are soft. Stir in the paprika and add the meat with the water in which it was washed still on it. Salt it, give it a screw of black pepper, and mix well. Add the chilli. Cook uncovered until the meat is tender, adding a little liquid as and when you need to.

Mix the soured cream with the flour, pour it into the pan and give it one stir (thereafter, only shake it – you are trying to create a marbled effect). Add the sausage, just dabbing it under the surface. Cook for 5 minutes more. If you like, garnish with slices of tomato, sweet pepper, chopped parsley and more soured cream.

# PAKISTAN

'Zia names day for elections but bans all political parties.'
Headline in *The Times*, January 1985

For all its sunshine, Pakistan is one of the world's darker places; and the face of democracy has been in purdah there for more years than it is comfortable to remember. It is in a sensitive position, for it has borders with Iran and its fundamentalists, Afghanistan and its Russian invaders, China and its Communists. It boasts a military dictator permanently on a political high-wire, and a programme to develop a nuclear bomb; it has poverty, hunger, corruption, disease and injustice. Alas for all India, none of these is anything new, except for the bomb; but the people have a tradition of endurance, hard work, hospitality even in hardship, and cheerfulness in chaos – establishing small islands of personal life and organisation in an anarchic sea of people.

Pakistan may be a new country, set up as a home for the Muslim dream when the British left India (the Sunni Muslims are the dominant group); but its history is as a rather special part of the whole subcontinent. Pakistan was the setting for one of the world's most ancient civilisations, that of the Indus valley. It was also the place where the invaders came into the subcontinent – the first, the Aryans, twelve or fifteen hundred years before Christ, when the Indus civilisation had been in existence for a thousand years. and perhaps had already crumbled. Looking at the ordered town planning of that civilisation forgotten for millennia, it is difficult to avoid the thought that many nearby people today live worse. (However, it is doubtful whether civilisation ever saved anyone from destruction.)

The Aryans were only the first, to be followed by Persians, Greeks and Arabs. Babur, the first Mongol (or Mughal) emperor, was following in his forefathers' footsteps when he established his dynasty: Timur the lame, Marlowe's Tamburlaine the Great, had invaded a hundred years before, and Babur's ancestor on his mother's side, Jenghiz Khan, had got as far as the Indus. The talents of this agreeable family of marauders were not limited to blinding their relatives, impaling their followers, building towers of severed human heads and getting extremely high on hash or booze (their Muslim faith notwithstanding). They had some areas of cultivation which, if evinced by any of our leaders today, would make us think the skies had fallen. Babur, for instance, recorded all the flora, fauna and even sociology of his new conquest of Hindustan in the illuminated autobiography which he kept honestly and obsessionally. He was a great bird-watcher. He was also a great maker of gardens.

With Humayun and Akbar the Great, a contemporary of England's first Elizabeth, began two centuries of splendour. Where Babur had sometimes had nothing but a tent, his descendants made palaces. Where he had once carried his culture with him in the form of a few books and precious objects, they put their splendour on the walls — with elaborate mosaics and halls of myriad mirrors — or sat upon it in the form of the jewelled Peacock Throne.

They also ate it: and even today, people in India and Pakistan put silver leaf on their food at the drop of a special occasion — beaten extremely thin and very low in calories, but pure silver nevertheless. From a present-day wedding feast in Lahore come two kingly dishes — a chicken *biryani* and a *kofta* curry with an extremely worrying idea behind it.

# LAHORE

*'The weddings. The birthdays. The funerals. There were always crowds . . . the city streets full of crowds.'* Ruth Prawer Jhabvala, *Autobiography of a Princess*

People like Lahore. Capital of the rich Western Punjab, which supplies Pakistan with a high proportion of its soldiers and administrators, its bazaars throb with colour and activity; and its Red Fort, Badshahi Mosque and tombs of Jehangir and his empress Nurjehan are not the only buildings so remarkable that it is rather difficult to believe in them at all. There is also a cathedral by Gilbert Scott, a Charing Cross and a Mall.

A *biryani* is a rice dish in which the rice is made to absorb other flavours, such as meat, butter and spices, and, apart from containing more better-quality materials than the less elaborate *pulao*, it is more decorated and coloured. The wedding-feast *biryani* was prepared by two ladies scarcely less attractive and decorated, who rattled a good deal with bangles, wore long red-enamelled fingernails and had some difficulty in keeping their saris out of the condiments.

They began by grinding the spices. Old herbs and spices of any kind are never a good idea, but in a cuisine where they are of such importance people become very particular about their freshness. Of course, it is much easier to have exotic spices always in perfect condition if you buy them fresh in the first place and get through them at such a rate that they never have a chance to go stale. One of the many assets immigrants have brought to Britain is the ready availability of authentic Indian foods. British Indian curry powder has a charm of its own, but no place in a dish like this; nor has the standard *garam masala* mixture. In Indian cooking, the use of spices and herbs is highly developed: it may be strong, subtle, or both, but it is never random, being originally based on a medicinal logic, among other things.

Some flavourings (usually seeds) are hard and dry and grind to a powder; others (tending to be roots and fruits) are softer and wetter and grind to a paste, so each kind is dealt with separately before you start to cook. When the roots and fruits are ready prepared commercially they often become powders – ginger and turmeric roots are examples of this. Powdered ginger changes its character significantly, and should not be substituted for fresh ginger except in desperation; but turmeric is hardly ever found as anything but a powder in Britain.

Red chilli powder is like the whole dried chilli – something to be careful of; and it is not a substitute for fresh green chillies (which may or may not have begun to turn red). Different types of green chillies have different heats – the long pointy one commonly available in Britain is much hotter than the short shiny one found less frequently. The more seeds you use, the hotter. My personal preference is for de-seeding fresh chillies before use, and quite often blanching them so that I can use more of them to increase the amount of chilli flavour without too much heat. (Note: if you have been cutting chillies and stick your finger up your nose, in your eye or any other sensitive area of your person, everybody around you will have a Real Laugh.)

Of the other spices: cardamoms are generally either small and green (occasionally white) or large, hairy and brown; the tiny delicious seeds known as Grains of Paradise are a rarity. Cumin seeds also fall into two main categories: green (or white) and black. Poppy seeds are white, not the black specks with which our bakers ornament our bread. Saffron is expensive (hardly surprising, with over 1000 crocuses to the ounce) and needs to be soaked in warm water, a pinch at a time. Cloves may be bought ground, and an ounce of whole fenugreek is like an ounce of gravel (attempting to pound it in a pestle and mortar is a memorable experience), so that is usually bought ground too. Other spices should be bought whole, and are sometimes first lightly roasted (not burnt) in a dry frying pan to bring out the flavour before they are ground. A coffee-grinder will do the job nicely, and impart an interesting flavour to your coffee for several cups following. This is quite authentic, for a little crushed cardamom is often added to coffee in the Middle East, but less aromatic spirits may wish to go back to the Stone Age with a separate pestle and mortar.

The experienced cook works by instinct in choosing quantities of spices, so the proportions given are really no more than a record of a particular occasion; but in judging flavour, remember that Pakistani cooking is spiced less strongly than South Indian. (In this book, spice quantities tend to be rounded down.)

Rice is critical. With pudding rice you cannot make anything but rice pudding, and British rice pudding does not occupy an exalted place in the universe. 'Long-grain' is the magic description, and it may be called *basmati*, though this is only one possible name. The rice used in Indian cooking is usually polished rather than brown. In the wedding *biryani* the rice is parboiled beforehand, but *biryanis* are also made with uncooked rice and with rice that has been totally pre-cooked.

But the chicken seems to be hardly cooked at all: just to warm through in the rice. While this steaming (a technique which is called *dum*) is particularly effective because the pot is so tightly sealed, almost as if it were a low-pressure cooker, the real secret is in the marinade. It contains papaya, which tenderises the meat almost to the extent of pre-digesting it. Here again the original recipe is alarming: for it asks for only 10 minutes in the marinade for chicken, and 30 minutes for lamb. Even to this, however, there is a logic: because papain (the enzyme that breaks down the meat very similarly to pepsin in the stomach) works best at $60°-79°C$ ($140°-175°F$) – just the sort of temperature provided by a pot of rice warming over a low heat.

Nevertheless, I still prefer to marinate for an hour or more – and not in the fridge. I prick the meat well so that the papain can get inside, and make the pieces no thicker than a chicken-breast. I use fresh, not frozen chicken. Then the recipe works well – but be very careful not to overcook the rice.

# CHICKEN BIRYANI
## (*Murgh Biryani*)
MRS ZUBAIDA TARIQ AND MISS HUMA SIRAJ, IN LAHORE

ENOUGH FOR 10 TO 15 PEOPLE

---

1 teaspoon saffron filaments, crushed, or $\frac{1}{2}$ teaspoon powder

1 kg ($2\frac{1}{4}$ lb) fresh chicken, cut up into fairly small pieces

250 g (9 oz) onions, sliced

750 g (1 lb 10 oz) clarified butter for deep-frying

1 kg ($2\frac{1}{4}$ lb) rice

6 pieces of cinnamon bark

6 small cardamoms

6 cloves

10 black peppercorns

Juice of 1 lemon

2 or more green chillies, de-seeded and chopped

$\frac{1}{2}$ handful each of mint and coriander (or other herbs), chopped

Flour and water paste

---

*Garnish* (optional)

Silver leaf

---

*Marinade*

25 g (1 oz) each of black pepper and poppy seeds, ground

10 g ($\frac{1}{2}$ oz) each large cardamoms, small cardamoms, black cumin seeds, ground

7 cm (3 inch) cinnamon stick, ground

3 cloves, ground

$\frac{1}{2}$ handful each mint and coriander leaves, chopped

20 g (1 oz) almonds, ground

2 green chillies, chopped

25 g (1 oz) fresh ginger, chopped

25 g (1 oz) garlic, crushed

1 teaspoon red chilli powder (or to taste)

Salt

25 g (1 oz) papaya, finely chopped

750 ml ($1\frac{1}{4}$ pints) yogurt

---

PREPARATION: Put the saffron to soak in a little warm water. Prick the chicken pieces all over. Combine the spices and other flavourings for the marinade and toss the meat in them well. Add the yogurt and mix that well in too. Leave the chicken to marinate for at least an hour in a warm place.

Set a large pan of salted water to boil. Deep-fry the onions in the clarified butter until brown. Strain them, keeping the butter. When they are cool, crumble them. Put the rice in the boiling water together with 1 tablespoon of the butter, the pieces of cinnamon bark and the whole cardamoms, cloves and peppercorns. Three-quarters cook the rice until the grains are only slightly hard, but will not crush completely between the fingers (this will probably take about 10 minutes). Drain it well. In a large saucepan, layer the rice and the chicken, colouring parts of the rice with saffron water and sprinkling with lemon juice, crumbled onion, bits of chilli, chopped mint and coriander, and the butter in which the onions were browned. Seal the pan with a flour and water paste and cook slowly, either on a fireproof mat set over a low heat or in a low oven (150°C, 300°F, gas mark 2), for 30 to 45 minutes. Decorate with silver leaf.

For myself, I have always thought that silver leaf makes the plate look a bit like a scrapyard: but beauty is in the eye of the beholder. Except at a Pakistani wedding, where it is in the Eye of the Beloved – for that is the name of a ceremonial meatball instantly recognisable as a Pakistani Scotch egg. The way to a bridegroom's heart may be through his stomach, but I do not find the name appealing to my romantic sensibilities, even when the egg is compared to a narcissus, as it sometimes is. In terms of eating, though, I would rather have this than a Scotch egg any day.

# THE EYE OF THE BELOVED
## (*Nargisi Kofta*)
MRS ZUBAIDA TARIQ AND MISS HUMA SIRAJ, LAHORE

MAKES 12 MEATBALLS

| |
|---|
| 100 g (4 oz) onions, sliced |
| 500 g (1 lb 2 oz) lamb or beef, minced |
| 100 g (4 oz) flour |
| 25 g (1 oz) each poppy seeds, white cumin, black pepper, ground |
| 25 g (1 oz) poppy seeds, ground |
| A good pinch of fennel seed, ground |
| 10 g ($\frac{1}{2}$ oz) small cardamoms, ground |
| 2 cloves, ground |
| 25 g (1 oz) almonds, ground |
| 1 tablespoon mint, finely chopped |
| 2 tablespoons coriander, finely chopped |
| 1 green chilli, finely chopped |
| 13 eggs, 12 hard-boiled and shelled |
| Juice of $\frac{1}{2}$ lemon |
| Red chilli powder |
| Salt |
| Clarified butter for deep-frying |
| *Sauce* |
| 25 g (1 oz) garlic |
| 25 g (1 oz) ginger |
| 1 teaspoon red chilli powder (or to taste) |
| $\frac{1}{2}$ teaspoon turmeric |
| Salt |
| 250 g (9 oz) onions, sliced |
| 375 g (13 oz) clarified butter for frying |
| 570 ml (1 pint) yogurt |

PREPARATION: Grind the sauce spices together to a paste. Deep-fry all the onions (for the meatballs and for the sauce) in clarified butter. Take out about 100 g (4 oz) for the meatballs. Mix the flavouring paste in with the sauce onions and continue frying for a few moments, then stir in the yogurt. Leave the sauce to simmer until the yogurt separates and dries out.

Crumble the onions for the meatballs. Mix well with the minced meat, the flour, the ground meatball spices, the ground almonds, the crumbled onion, the chopped mint, coriander and chillies, the raw egg and the lemon juice. Add red chilli powder and salt to taste. Form each meatball by patting some of the mixture flat in the palm of one hand and wrapping it round an egg. Fry in plenty of clarified butter, over a moderate heat. Carefully cut each meatball in half. Serve in the sauce.

The beloved's eye twinkles briefly. Family eating is less elaborate than moghul *biryanis*, but its basic dishes are perhaps even more worthy of respect, with cheap ingredients making savoury and practical dishes, including a range of breads that start with the simplest possible doughs. *Chapatis* are simply wholemeal flour fairly well-kneaded with a little salt and water – left to rest for half an hour, made into balls, rolled out, roasted on a griddle and puffed by briefly holding it over a flame. For stuffed *parathas*, two raw *chapatis* are lightly buttered with *ghee*, dotted with any combination of filling that needs little extra cooking – boiled cauliflower, potato, or spinach, cooked meat or lentils – and a seasoning of chopped onion, green chillies, chilli-powder and chopped coriander leaves, before being rolled out together, filling and all, and being browned on both sides in *ghee*.

*Puri* is more sophisticated: and, with a vegetable curry and *halwa* (buttery semolina pudding), is bacon and eggs, toast and marmalade in Pakistan.

At the stall, the cook works wonders with a wok of oil, a spatula, a *karhai* (a hemispherical bowl which is really a deep-fryer but which he uses as a mixing vessel) and a pair of hands. No rolling pin – he rolls some dough into a ball, squashes it, and bats it back and forth between his palms until it turns into a thin pancake the size of a saucer. A nonchalant toss into the hot oil – pat it down, turn it over, baste it, take it out – and there is a puffy pancake to rival the lightest *crêpe* a Frenchman ever made. (Nor did the great Escoffier have to work squatting on his haunches.)

At home this simple business somehow becomes less so, and you are likely to find yourself having to use a rolling pin: or otherwise, the secrets of *puri* reveal themselves with practice.

# PUFFY PANCAKES
## *(Puri)*
### MR MOHAMMAD RIAZ, AT A FOOD-STALL IN LAHORE
### RECKON ON 2 *PURIS* PER 25 G (1 OZ) FLOUR

| |
| --- |
| **1 part strong wholemeal flour** |
| **3 parts strong white flour** |
| **Salt** |
| **Water** |
| **A little clarified butter, and clarified butter or oil for deep-frying** |

PREPARATION: Mix the flours and salt together. Add water progressively and knead to make a softish but resilient dough. Knead well, preferably for 10 minutes or more.

Rub clarified butter on the top of the lump of dough: knead, turn over, and knead again. Break off small pieces of dough and roll them into balls about the size of a ping-pong ball. Let them have a brief rest, say half an hour.

Heat a few inches of clarified butter or oil in a pan or wok to a medium-high temperature (always make sure that a wok used for deep-frying is properly supported).

One by one, roll (or pat) out each ball of dough into a thin disc several inches across: put it into the frying fat, pat it once on top to push it under, wait a second or two for it to puff up, turn it over, splash oil over it for a few seconds with the spatula until it has puffed up again, take it out and drain on kitchen paper.

*Puri* is the kind of fried marvel in which fast-food places all over the world excel – based on simple ingredients, a repetitive demand and a professional technique that can be learned by those who may never know, or care, anything else about cooking. When fast-food cooks turn their hands to other things, the results are usually neither subtle nor precise.

*Aaloo Chana*, a curry of chick peas and potatoes, is quite a shock at breakfast time in terms of its quantity of chilli powder. I quote it as made on the stall because it is a useful and cheap vegetable curry which shows a basic method; but on the first attempt I would reduce the amount of chilli powder by at least half, and see how it suits your particular powder and your particular tastebuds. You might want to use less salt, too.

# CHICK PEA AND POTATO CURRY
## (*Aaloo Chana*)
### MR MOHAMMAD RIAZ, AT A FOOD-STALL IN LAHORE
### ENOUGH FOR 2 to 4 PEOPLE

| |
|---|
| **250 g (9 oz) chick peas that have been soaked overnight** |
| **1 onion, sliced** |
| **Clarified butter for frying** |
| **Salt** |
| **2 heaped teaspoons red chilli powder** |
| **1 heaped teaspoon turmeric** |
| **2.5 cm (1 inch) piece of fresh ginger, grated** |
| **1 or 2 green chillies, de-seeded and halved** |
| **2 tomatoes, chopped** |
| **450 g (1 lb) potatoes, parboiled and diced** |
| **Black pepper, black and white cumin, cinnamon, black cardamom, all ground (optional)** |

PREPARATION: Drain the chick peas, and boil them in salted water (adding other flavourings, if you like) till just cooked (about 2 to 3 hours).

Start browning the sliced onions in clarified butter and when they begin to colour add 3 heaped teaspoons of salt, the red chilli powder, and the turmeric. Fry them for a minute or two in the butter, then add the ginger, the green chillies and the tomatoes and cook for 2 to 3 minutes more. Add a cup of water (or a little more), the chick peas and the potatoes. Cook uncovered until the liquid has gone and serve hot, sprinkled with some of the optional spices.

Chick peas also make a flour, *channa* or *gram* flour, which is the flour used for *pakoras*, vegetable fritters. This imprecise recipe is a real free-for-all: practically any kind of vegetable can be used in any combination provided that it is not too watery, though potatoes, for instance, usually need pre-cooking. The seasoning too is largely a matter of taste.

The main things to be careful of are the standard fritter injunctions: get the oil temperature right (drop in a morsel of batter and see how it behaves) and do not crowd the pan. These apart, there should be no problems once you have got over the idea of mixing the fritter batter round the ingredients instead of separately. They are good party nibbles (or, rather, mouthfuls) and can be three-quarters cooked and finished off at the last moment if necessary (this makes them crisper, darker and greasier).

# SPICY VEGETABLE FRITTERS
## (*Pakoras*)
### MRS ZOHRA RAB NAWAZ, LAHORE
### MAKES 20 TO 30 PAKORAS

| |
|---|
| Clarified butter or oil for deep frying |
| 100 g ($\frac{1}{4}$ lb) each spinach and cabbage, cut into pieces about 2.5 cm (1 inch) across |
| 100 g ($\frac{1}{4}$ lb) potatoes, parboiled and diced |
| 100 g ($\frac{1}{4}$ lb) cauliflower, divided into florets |
| 100 g ($\frac{1}{4}$ lb) onions, roughly chopped |
| 100 g ($\frac{1}{4}$ lb) sweet peppers, cut into chunks |
| Some mint and coriander leaves, roughly chopped |
| A few green chillies, chopped fairly small |
| Salt |
| Red chilli powder |
| $\frac{1}{4}$ teaspoon baking powder |
| 2 tablespoons oil |
| 700 g ($1\frac{1}{2}$ lb) *gram* flour |
| About 1 litre ($1\frac{3}{4}$ pints) water |

PREPARATION: Heat the clarified butter or oil to medium-hot.

Mix all the vegetables and seasonings together in a bowl, then scatter the baking powder over and mix the 2 tablespoons of oil well in. Add the flour, mixing it in handful by handful, and when it is all in begin to add water, mixing all the time until you arrive at a fritter batter which is wet enough to enclose everything properly but not so wet that it falls apart.

Take bits of the mixture about 5 cm (2 inches) across and deep-fry them, not so many at a time that you reduce the temperature of the oil, until they are golden brown. Drain well. They will hang around a bit if they must, but they are better hot.

Being good party food, *pakoras* are apt to turn up at the Feast of Alms, Id-us-sadaqah, which ends the month's fasting between dawn and dusk of Ramadhan. But the dish that always features at Id-us-sadaqah is a sweet noodle pudding, *siwayian*, which is a traditional gift between friends on that day.

*Siwayian* uses *khoya*, which is the dairy equivalent of a stock cube – rich milk boiled down until it becomes a solid. We have no Western equivalent – the nearest thing would be unsweetened condensed milk or powdered milk (it may have been what the Burgundian chef making Pear Charlotte was searching for when he added powdered milk to his pear juice); but making it is no problem for those with a placid and persevering temperament, since it only involves boiling carefully and stirring to make sure that the milk neither inundates the stove nor burns. The process provides a good opportunity for having beautiful, and rather long, thoughts: it takes up to two hours, for which your reward is something rather more solid and more natural-tasting than condensed milk and a slight sensation of achievement.

There are many recipes for *siwayian* – this is a rather elaborate one, prepared in a modern kitchen by Mrs Zohra Rab Nawaz, a grey-haired lady who cooks on Pakistan television. Her local noodles were dry, in short lengths, very thin (a little stouter than Chinese cellophane noodles), and golden.

# NOODLE PUDDING
## (*Siwayian*)
### MRS ZOHRA RAB NAWAZ, LAHORE
### ENOUGH FOR 6 TO 8 PEOPLE

| |
|---|
| **Seeds of 4 or 5 small cardamoms** |
| **100 g (4 oz) butter** |
| **About 250 g (9 oz) vermicelli or other thin noodles, broken into 8 cm (3 inch) lengths** |
| **1 litre (1¾ pints) milk** |
| **100 g (4 oz) *khoya* (concentrate of 1 litre/1¾ pints Jersey milk or ½ tin unsweetened condensed milk)** |
| **A pinch of saffron, in a little warm water** |
| **Sugar** |
| **3 or 4 fresh dates or soaked dried dates, shredded** |
| **12 almonds, blanched and shredded** |
| **12 pistachio nuts, shredded** |
| ***Garnish* (optional)** |
| **Silver leaf** |

PREPARATION: Fry the cardamom seeds in the butter until they smell fragrant. Add the noodles and toss over a low heat, making sure that they do not burn, until they have taken some colour. Take them off the heat and pour in the milk. Return to a moderate heat to cook until soft.

Add the *khoya* and some saffron water (remembering that too much saffron can be bitter). Add sugar to taste. When the mixture has thickened to something like hot custard, stir in the dates and most of the shredded almonds and pistachios, reserving some of the nuts for decoration. Pour into a bowl and decorate with shredded nuts and, if you have it, silver leaf. Serve hot or cold, with or without cream.

〜 • 〜

The same milk-*khoya*-cardamom-sugar-saffron mixture with dates and nuts is also cooked (without noodles) until it begins to thicken and then poured over slices of bread fried golden in clarified butter: this is *Shahi Tukra*, The King's Titbit. Back to the Mongols again.

# THE FRONTIER

*'If you see a cow you have found water; if you see a donkey you have found a camp; if you see a camel you are lost.'* Saying in Baluchistan

The western frontier of Pakistan perpetuates other, tougher Mongol qualities — warrior fierceness in the north, the nomadic way of life further south. Though there are prosperous orchards near Quetta where the camel route comes in, much of Baluchistan province is arid and the traditional way of life is nomadic. They have a simple way of barbecuing sheep and goats. The animals are jointed and salted, and a long skewer is run lengthwise down each of the limbs. The ends of the skewers are simply driven into the ground in a line, and brushwood fires are built either side one or two paces from the meat, which will be done in anything between two and five hours and, with luck, will taste not only of the smoke but of the desert aromatics gathered with the fuel. Longer cooking further away from the fire is generally thought better.

Travellers in the desert receive great hospitality — for in the desert to send men away from your tent may be to send them to their deaths — but when the traveller asks for bread, he is also given a stone. The desert bread, *kak*, is made around an open fire: stones are heated, the dough is rolled round them, and the whole lot is put to bake near the embers for 30 minutes to an hour. The result is extremely iron rations, even with the loaf cracked open and the stone thrown away; but it keeps.

It is undeniable that the men of the North-West Frontier are impressive: anyone is, with a bandolier of that many bullets; and the knowledge that many of the rifles are homemade makes you fear for the owners as much as anyone else. But the pride and courage of the tribesmen endeared them even to the British colonialists to whom they gave so much trouble. The two sides killed each other, more or less horribly, but respected each other while they did it.

The tribes were never conquered, nor are they now in these mountains which are sometimes the Himalayas, sometimes the Karakorum, sometimes the Hindu Kush – but always a law unto themselves. British or no British, Zia or no Zia, Russians or no Russians, off the road old rules apply.

The travellers in this region not only wear sandals but eat them: for *chappli* is their name both for their footwear and for the robust rissole accompanying the big bread pancake or *nan* whose fragrance fills the roadside cafés. Baked in clay ovens in the ground (*tandoors*), these *nan* are the size of two dinner plates put together, and textured with the knuckles so that they look quilted. The *chappli*, as flat as a sandal, is cooked in a round pan several feet across and tilted at one end so that the fat collects there, over the heat. The cook sits at the cool end, pushes the ingredients over to fry with the flat of his hand, brings them back to keep warm: an excellent example of ergonomics.

*Chappli kabaab* ought really to be made out of buffalo meat and fried in buffalo fat, but the absence of a neighbourhood buffalo-butcher need not inhibit you from making them out of any kind of mince you like. They are in no way subtle, and the spices are more crushed than ground, even the red chillies.

# CHAPPLI KABAAB
## A CAFÉ IN THE NORTH-WEST FRONTIER PROVINCE
### MAKES 16 KABAABS

| |
|---|
| 2 kg (4½ lb) beef or lamb, finely minced |
| 450 g (1 lb) maize flour |
| Salt |
| 450 g (1 lb) onions, diced |
| 450 g (1 lb) tomatoes, roughly chopped |
| 100 g (4 oz) green chillies, chopped |
| 100 g (4 oz) each red chillies, white cumin seeds, coriander seeds, dried pomegranate seeds, crushed |
| 8 eggs |
| Beef dripping or clarified butter for frying |

PREPARATION: Mix the meat with the maize flour and salt to taste. Mix in all the vegetables and spices. Whoosh the eggs about in the dripping to half-fry them, keeping them soft. Mix them into the meat mixture.

Pat into flat rissoles about the size of a small hand and fry in just enough dripping to cover until the edges are just about to crisp, but the middle is still soft.

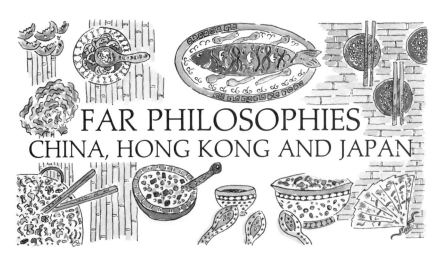

# FAR PHILOSOPHIES
## CHINA, HONG KONG AND JAPAN

With the Far East it becomes difficult – and perhaps inappropriate – to talk of food in the personal terms that can be used of Western countries. It is no longer a question of variations on a theme: the tune itself has changed. In the West, we all play solos and think that we make a great noise; but in China and Japan society is a mighty orchestra. (Even in Hong Kong, it is a Big Band.)

Because these societies are so different from ours, they have most to teach us. We can find new dishes nearer home: but in the East we can find new principles – not to replace our own, but to enrich them. If they sometimes seem strange, we should be adventurous. For even if one end of the Oriental gullet is a stomach not quite the same as a Western one in its tolerances of alcohol and dairy fats, the tastebuds at the other just happen to have been educated in a different way. Anybody who cares to be, can be educated – or re-educated.

## China

*There are more ways of westernising Chinese*
*Than the variety of fishes in the seas:*
*It is extremely creditable as a profusion,*
*But is liable to result in a certain amount of confusion.*

Chinese cooking today is mainly divided north and south, Beijing and Guang-dong (Peking and Canton); and its other divisions include a broad distinction between east and west, the west being known for hot, spicy foods, while the east is good at vegetables and fish. That is a very simple summary of an enormous subject which also includes the preferences of no fewer than fifty-five ethnic minorities.

A quarter of the people in the world are Chinese, and a Chinese province may be as big as a sizeable European country. China is awe-inspiring – in its antiquity, its size, its rivers, its mountains, its numbers of people and the endurance of those people – the only nation to have withstood two and a half thousand years of bureaucracy and come out of it comparatively unscathed (apart from an assortment of floods, famines, invasions, earthquakes, dynasties, revolutions and other natural and unnatural disasters). Its twentieth-century history has been entirely in keeping with its past – prodigious both in suffering and in efforts to make life better for its people.

China's cooking is awe-inspiring, too: for those who are not blasé about extracting the emerald-green contents of the gall-bladder of a poisonous snake and drinking it; or making a relish out of wasps; or consuming the dried ovaries of the Manchurian Tree Frog. As for camel hump – why, you can buy it deep-frozen in Hong Kong. (It is extremely fatty and, they say, overrated.) Birds' nests and sharks' fins are regular status symbols at banquets – both eaten for their gelatinous texture, rather than their flavour. Dog is less eaten nowadays, but tortoise is thought particularly healthy eating. Snake's flesh is a delicacy.

An omnivorous diet is sometimes said to be the result of poverty and indeed nothing encourages a varied diet like the pangs of hunger. In the same way, shortage of fuel is one reason for the wok: stir-frying is very economical of energy. But another reason for the prevalence of the wok in China is that it is one of the most ingenious pieces of kitchen equipment ever, as well as one of the simplest. And a cuisine as sophisticated as the Chinese is not the sort of thing that results from bare necessity, or that is invented by the poor. There is peasant food in China, as there is in the West; and even in today's egalitarian society, the number of Peking Ducks consumed per year by an agricultural labourer is extremely small but the court, nobility and merchants had other things on their mind than starvation – how to make their meals refined, novel, splendid; and, being Chinese and (often) Taoist (Daoist) – how to eat in a way that was artistically and philosophically satisfying.

However you feel about Taoism in the cosmic sense, it is a good basis for a system of cooking. The idea of a harmony of contrasts – the moon and sun, female and male principles of *yin* and *yang* – is exactly what a great deal of cooking is about, though, like any other principle, it can also be rubbish in the wrong hands; and even in the right ones, the detailed classification of many foods on a scale between 100 per cent hot *yang* and 100 per cent cold *yin* may be a bureaucratic exercise you would prefer to ignore. Such a system encourages both simplicity and variety; and it makes people discriminate. Furthermore, being a system of medicine as well as of cookery, it promotes healthy eating. Westerners may regret that it does not encourage the flowering of individual talent and personality; but this may be our aberration, not theirs.

Buddhism has also influenced Chinese cooking. Buddhism values life, so it is vegetarian, but more than that: it values not only the lives of animals but also the rest of Creation. It is a Chinese tradition to accord even quite humble household objects the dignity of a ceremony when they are worn out, as if they were people, who ought to have funerals. Outside monasteries, however, 'vegetarian' does not necessarily mean what it does in the West, and vegetarians of conscience may find ethical surprises on the menus of China's vegetarian restaurants.

# Beijing

*'A sour spring, a bitter summer, a spicy autumn, a salty winter — these, with smooth and sweet, are the seasonings of the year.'* Li Ji, *The Book of Rites*, fourth century BC

The cuisine of China goes back some half a million years, to the time when Peking Man enjoyed his Sunday roasts — except, of course, that he did not know it was Sunday. Peking Man himself no longer exists — at least publicly — having been lost by the Americans when they attempted to get him out of the country during the war with Japan. It is the final straw in an existence which cannot have been easy, since in his day Beijing winters were even colder than they are now, when the chill has to be kept out with goatskin coats, and there would have been the same sandstorms off the Gobi desert in January and February. (They have a pudding of chestnuts and candied fruit named after them, the dust being the spun sugar that covers it.)

Beijing was once Yanjing, the Swallow Capital. Its present name means Northern Peace, and this is the town that — with the help of the Great Wall some fifty miles away — sometimes managed to keep it. However, the modern city began as the capital of an invader, the Mongol emperor Kubilai Khan. In those days Beijing was a city of wide streets, great halls and parks, and it is rather like that again today, though the Great Khan and most of his works are gone, except for a few of the parks. It was an onion of exclusivity in its days as the Imperial City — Outer, Inner, Imperial and Forbidden Cities, with the Emperor at the centre; but nowadays the city spreads and lays a concrete hand upon the old jumble of alleys and houses, hiding the tatty blankness of their courtyard walls.

Beijing amply expresses the vastness of the country whose capital it is. Its

China: Sautéed Roast Duck Slices and Lettuce page 143

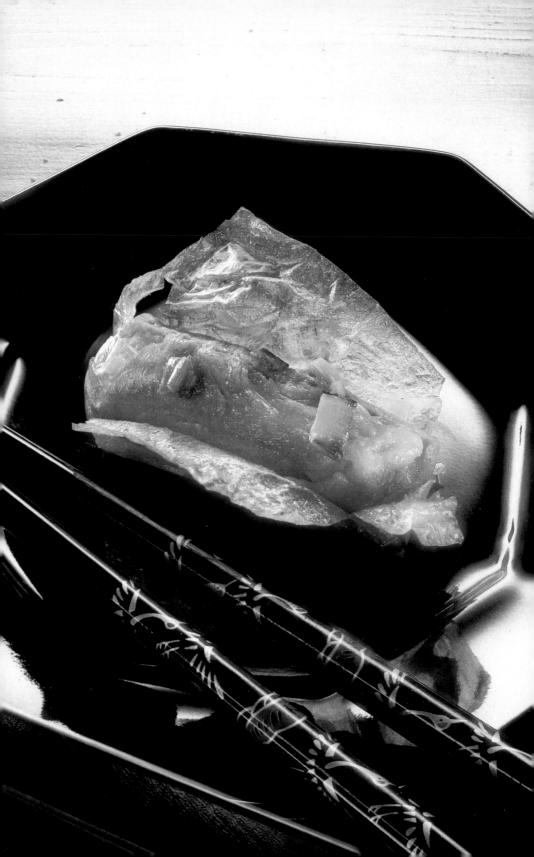

high street, Chang'an Avenue, runs twenty-five miles east to west with a carillon of bicycle bells all the way. Greater Beijing is ninety miles across at its widest, and beneath it all runs the network of tunnels and nuclear shelters that present-day China has built under every major city. Tianan men Square, with its Monument to the People's Heroes, is nearly 100 acres, enough to hold a crowd one-million strong. (What on earth, one wonders, do they all do for public lavatories?)

The great halls of today include not only the Mao Memorial and the Great Hall of the People, but the Roast Duck Restaurants. Beijing Quangjude contains 41 dining rooms, and a staff of 600 caters for 2500 customers at once. It is a Western-sixties-style building, with rather more glass and rather less concrete than many: for places of public resort in China often have an ambience not unlike that of a DHSS office. When the Chinese stop being folksy or artistic or historical, and start to be modern, they seem as yet to be unable to find an aesthetic.

Peking Duck itself is imperial in scale. It was a royal recipe from the Mongols, prodigal of fuel in a country which developed stir-frying because it never had enough wood to heat ovens; and the original recipe itself is vast — extending to some 15,000 words. The Quangjude duck, which is raised at Mount Jade Spring outside Beijing in similar conditions to the Strasbourg goose, not only provides a roast, or the roast with Chinese pancakes, spring onions, crispy skin and Hoi Sin sauce that we know in Britain as Peking Duck, but an entire banquet, beginning with picture-plates of hors-d'œuvres.

On a white table-cloth in a quiet room, a young chef, Wan Tongli, worked with a gold-handled knife preparing Pine and Crane Promise Longevity from slices of pickled duck, cherries, cocoa powder and other colourings, agar, star jelly and crab. There was a tendency for the pine to look like an aquatic rhubarb, but this is a matter of artistic licence and the Chinese taste in pine trees. Of the four cranes with white-meat plumage and cherry-coloured caps, one was picking its toenails with its beak, two were flying upside down, and one was standing on one leg trying to work out why. How they would have appeared to a bird-watcher is uncertain: but to anyone else they looked as if they were part of a plate which had been enamelled and which had strange crane-shaped bumps — for there was quite a reasonable amount of meat on them.

On the plate next door, two dumpy Magpies on a Plum Tree were celebrating the coming of spring with brown branches, red flowers, and a complicated Chinese word in puce. Two goldfish had duck-meat bodies, duck-web tails and staring cherry eyes: they might well look surprised — they had

Hong Kong: Spare Ribs in Paper page 159

just encountered a tomato twice as big as themselves and cut like a flower. Crowing Cock in the Morning lacked nothing but his crow. Pandas Pleasing Among the Bamboos, being pandas, were pleasing in a perfectly respectable manner, lying around munching leaves.

Why do they bother with this extravagant approach to *haute cuisine*? Eating is important to the Chinese; there is a tradition; and China has a policy of full employment, so that if a new machine can put a man out of work it may be the machine that goes. Most important, the craftsman is prized. In old China, the craftsmen, like the nobility, the peasants and the merchants, formed a distinct social class; and they ranked well above the merchants, who might be made to live outside the city walls with others who put money first, like the prostitutes. The contrast with our own civilisation is striking: we have under-valued, exploited and destroyed our craftsmen; and reserved our honours for those who never made anything but money.

Chinese chefs do not wear the tall chef's hat we are used to, and the Head Chef of the Quangjude, Cheng Shoubing, sported just the sort of floppy flat thing that Bohemian painters used to wear in Montmartre. In the tiled kitchens, rows of white-crowned artists tended rows of woks nestling in round holes in iron ranges that flamed and lit the fat when the food was tossed, as their particular contribution to the frenzy. Cheng worked at a hob about the size of a small cabin-cruiser, with a trough at the back, so that when he had finished with something in the wok he could simply throw it down the back of the stove – a sensible arrangement, but rather unnerving in its nonchalance.

Though there are restaurants in Peking which boast that they have had the same stockpot on the boil for up to two centuries, much of Chinese cooking is instant – everything prepared with great finesse, possibly for hours, then assembled in the wok in a few minutes (or even seconds). You have to think in advance and you have to be well organised. This, and the immensely ancient tradition, are probably why the cuisine has such clarity. When you do something, you always know why. Professional Chinese cooks have all their sauces to hand, out in pots: it makes for very efficient working.

The chopping board was a section of a tree with the bark still on, the knife a cleaver – a Chinese custom which has advantages, since it gives you the weight of a big knife without the length to slow you down. A Chinese chef does not cut with his cleaver – he engages it as a partner with which to dance on the ingredients. Perfect slices of breast of duck climbed up the blade; duck livers were sliced sideways to the thickness of a rasher of bacon. Webs of ducks' feet were split horizontally and trimmed. The meat was mostly pre-cooked, except for the innards. The Duck Feast is theoretically a way of using up all parts of the same roasted bird. In practice, such things as web and heart are in rather short supply on a duck, and to reproduce this duck feast you will need either an extravagant number of birds or extra quantities of the scarce bits. Most of these are not in demand in Britain, so a real butcher should be able to help you.

After the cranes, magpies, cock, goldfish and pandas pleasing of the artistic hors-d'œuvres, the dishes of this feast are: sautéed duck hearts; slices of duck with web and liver in fermented rice sauce; Beijing Duck Rolls (with pancakes, sauce and salad); Stewed Duck Four Delicacies (the tongue, breast, web and pancreas); and slices of roast duck sautéed with lettuce. (Duck soup is also served at the end of the meal.)

The crisply roasted skin of the duck is the ultimate delicacy of the meal. Often, before the duck is roasted, its skin is blown up, through a hole in the skin of the neck, to separate it from the meat. But there are alternatives to getting out your bicycle pump. The Cantonese method (see page 167) begins by putting the duck in boiling water. Some people rub gin, vodka or brandy into the skin and leave it to soak in for about three hours. Whatever the preliminaries, the essential process is the one that follows – coating the duck with a sweet wash, usually honey, and hanging it up to air-dry in a cool place for between four and twenty-four hours. Other birds can be treated in the same way. A duck will roast in about $1\frac{1}{4}$ to $1\frac{1}{2}$ hours, the first 15 to 30 minutes of which should be at a very high temperature (at least 230°C, 450°F, gas mark 8), the remainder at about 190°C (375°F, gas mark 5). It will need basting and, in the absence of a spit, turning – and turning carefully for fear of damaging the skin (hold it with a cloth).

The original marinade will please few people who have not already acquired a taste for the nuclear-powered Maotai wine (106° proof), since its character can only be politely described as gamey, verging on rottenness. (Even without distillation, rice wine can attain a fair strength, so always err in that direction when wine is called for in Chinese cooking.)

The top of each heart is chopped off, then the hearts are slit lengthways and opened out like fans, with cuts made almost through in the pattern of fan ribs. They are marinated for an hour or so in a mixture of Maotai wine (which you may prefer to replace with dry sherry or some sort of spirit, marc if available), soy sauce, sesame oil, chopped spring onions, coriander, salt, white pepper, sugar, and monosodium glutamate if you use it. The hearts are then briefly deep-fried in duck fat or oil.

Stewed Duck in Fermented Rice Sauce is really only for those in the habit of making rice wine, since the sauce appears to be no more than the lees of the fermentation (with rice wine you end up with a sloppy mess containing more alcohol than you wish to leave behind), with some soy sauce. The duck meat is mainly cooked breast and sliced duck liver, both of which are blanched before being stewed in a little stock with web from the feet. Duck feet can be bought cheaply by the frozen bagful from Chinese supermarkets in London. They are difficult to bone, and the ordinary cook will be limited to cutting out the web between the toes, which immediately shrinks to nothing. It does not seem to me to be worth the trouble.

Duck Rolls are another matter: they are meat wrapped in duck skin and deep-fried – easy for Western taste to accept. Once again, duckish conformity causes the creature to limit itself to one skin at a time, which means that you will not have enough skin to wrap all the meat. The Quangjude ducks are large, and the chefs there get about sixteen rolls per skin, but an average English duck will probably not provide more than a dozen of these crispy titbits.

# BEIJING DUCK ROLLS
### CHENG SHOUBING, QUANGJUDE RESTAURANT, BEIJING
### MAKES 12 TO 16 ROLLS

| |
|---|
| **1 duck (skin and leg-meat)** |
| **3 whole eggs** |
| **50 g (2 oz) flour** |
| **75 g (3 oz) breadcrumbs** |
| **Oil or duck fat for deep-frying** |
| *For the filling* |
| **2 slices of fresh ginger** |
| **6 to 8 water chestnuts** |
| **1 tablespoon wine (rice wine or dry sherry)** |
| **1 teaspoon seasame oil** |
| **$\frac{1}{2}$ teaspoon salt** |
| **Up to 1 teaspoon monsodium glutamate, if you insist** |
| **1 egg white** |
| *Garnish* |
| **Green vegetable (e.g. spinach, Chinese leaves, Pak-Choi, lettuce)** |

PREPARATION: Take the skin off the duck (a few cuts with a knife will help it to pull off quite easily, but with fat still attached). Cutting horizontally, slice as much of the fat as possible off the skin. Cook the skin in boiling water for about 10 minutes, and dry it.

Put the breasts aside, and mince the rest of the lean meat with the ginger. Chop the water chestnuts finely. Mix all the filling ingredients together.

Divide the cooked skin into squares about 6 cm (2½ inches) across, and roll up some filling in each. Turn the rolls in egg and flour and then in egg and breadcrumbs. Deep-fry them in a well-supported wok or a frying pan until they are golden brown and serve them on a bed of green vegetable (the vegetable used in the original dish was deep-fried slivers of rape, but any green vegetable, raw or quickly sautéed, should do).

In the Chinese kitchen, seasonings are much at the discretion of the cook, who will use salt, white pepper, wine, vinegar, soy and oyster sauce, sesame oil, fresh ginger and spring onion as well as more esoteric flavourings such as Sichuan (Szechuaun) peppercorns (pleasantly aromatic). Many also use monosodium glutamate, a habit which is every bit as charming and natural as replacing your lawn with green reinforced concrete.

# SAUTÉED ROAST DUCK SLICES AND LETTUCE

### CHENG SHOUBING, QUANGJUDE RESTAURANT, BEIJING

### IN COMBINATION WITH OTHER DISHES, ENOUGH FOR 4 PEOPLE

| |
|---|
| ½ roast duck |
| 1 crisp lettuce |
| 4 tablespoons groundnut or other light oil |
| 4 spring onions cut into 2·5 cm (1 inch) lengths |
| A selection of seasonings e.g. 2 teaspoons soy sauce; 2 teaspoons sesame oil; 1 tablespoon dry sherry; ¼ teaspoon white pepper; a good sprinkle of ground Sichuan peppercorns |
| 2 teaspoons cornflour blended with 2 teaspoons cold water |

PREPARATION: Put a pan of water on to boil. Slice the duck neatly and rather thinly, and halve the lettuce leaves lengthways. Blanch the lettuce leaves in the boiling water for an instant and drain.

Flavour the oil by frying the onions in it in a wok or frying pan over a medium heat, taking them out as they begin to brown. Mix the seasonings in a bowl and toss the meat and lettuce in them. Stir-fry the duck and lettuce together in the onion oil until the lettuce has wilted and the duck is hot. Pour the cornflour blend over, adjust the seasoning, and continue stir-frying for another minute.

There are other ritual meals to be had in Peking (indeed, wherever there are Chinese). Donglaishun by the East Wind market serves red-braised camel hump at four days' notice, but most people go there for the Hotpot.

You would not think that those who can take the hump would be choosy about other forms of meat: but there is a kind of morality about it among the general run of Chinese. Pork is the standard meat, fowl the minor delicacy, and many feel it somehow inappropriate to eat beef, since the ox is a beast of burden like our horse. The saying goes: 'The cow works; the pig is eaten; but the chicken is the poetry of a meal.' They do not even mention lamb, whose flesh they find rank, especially when older.

But the characters and religions of the ethnic minorities broaden the menu further. Lamb is eaten by the ten million Chinese Muslims, and in the north. Here, Mongolian influence was strong even before Kubilai Khan's dynasty. The Donglaishun traces Rinsed Mutton (which we usually prefer to call Mongolian Hotpot) back as far as Tang, China's golden age around the time of King Arthur; but it was an elemental dish for the nomadic Mongols; and the Qing (Ch'ing) court, the Manchurian dynasty that ruled China from the time of Cromwell, put it on their winter menu.

Mongolian Hotpot is a do-it-yourself dish like the Japanese *Shabu-shabu* and the Hong Kong Steamboat (which gets its name from the boiler with a central chimney which for all these dishes becomes the centrepiece of the table). Round the boiler is a trough which is filled with stock, in which everyone cooks their own meat, vegetables – and, in one case, the Chrysanthemum Fire Pot, even flowers. By the time everyone has had enough, the stock has been enriched by all the things that have been cooked in it, and can be drunk as soup: which is the right way round for China, which likes its soup at the end of a meal, not the beginning.

Like most simple ideas in cooking, all this is not quite so easy as it seems. The stock must be good. The meat must be thinly sliced with consummate skill or a good machine. With nothing more than a block and a large knife, an expert can produce meat through which you can see the pattern on the plate, each six inch slice weighing no more than a fifth of an ounce. He can cut two pounds of meat into 2000 slices, and produce 30,000 slices a day.

There is even a pitfall for the guests who, in some versions of this dish, mix their own dipping sauces from seven or eight bowls of ingredients on the table; and who are in danger of encountering the 'Well-it-tastes-awful-at-the-moment-but-I-think-I'll-just-try-a-bit-more-of-that-one ... Oh!-Well-it-tastes-awful-at ...' syndrome: which leaves them with a brimming bowl of something nasty. Perhaps it is all part of the fun of one of the few dishes that can be guaranteed to loosen a buttoned-up dinner party. But if you would rather play safer and provide ready-made sauces, Sesame Sauce and Pon-zu Sauce are on pages 176 and 177.

The lamb at the Donglaishun comes from the black-faced sheep raised in Inner Mongolia under the banner of West Wu. (Inner Mongolian local government has a heraldic quality to its administration, with leagues under commanders, tribes, and banners – a subdivision of the tribes – under hereditary chieftains.) It is best to choose a fairly lean piece of meat, the appreciation of boiled mutton fat being a rare science in Britain. The Chinese look upon fat as a delicacy, and cut each slice to include some. For Hotpot, the Chinese butcher prefers the chuck (shoulder and associated chops) and parts of the leg, but any cut that can be grilled or roasted will do, so long as it gives you a coherent slice with the amount of fat you want, cutting across the grain.

# RINSED MUTTON OR MONGOLIAN HOTPOT
## (*Shuan Yang Rou*)
DONGLAISHUN RESTAURANT, BEIJING

| |
|---|
| **Lamb** |
| **Good stock** |
| *Accompaniments* |
| **Cellophane noodles** |
| **Cabbage** |
| **Spinach** |
| **Pickled Chinese cabbage or other vegetables to taste** |
| **Beancurd** |
| **Cooked rice or dumplings** |
| *Condiments* |
| **Soy sauce** |
| **Sesame/chilli oils** |
| **Sesame paste** |
| **Shrimp sauce** |
| **Vinegar** |
| **Chive flowers** |
| *Soup ingredients* |
| **Chinese mushrooms** |
| **Dried shrimps** |
| **And you'll need a pot that can be kept simmering on the table** |

PREPARATION: Before cutting, trim the meat and half-freeze it (if it is possible to press the meat under a weight while you freeze it, so much the better). If you can, find a kindly soul with a bacon-slicer. Otherwise, the technique for cutting by hand needs a large knife with a rather convex edge. Held at an angle of about 30 degrees, it is gently bounced forward on to the meat, and raised again after every stroke to prevent the slice sticking to the blade.

Soak the cellophane noodles in warm water for a few minutes, until they are soft. Cut them up into manageable lengths and the vegetables into elegant pieces. Set out the accompaniments, and put out the condiments in individual bowls. Season the stock and preheat it. Add the mushrooms and dried shrimps.

Everyone cooks and makes their own bowl of seasoning sauce according to their fancy. The meat is done in a few seconds, when it turns colour. The cellophane noodles usually go into the soup at the end.

~ • ~

Chinese cooking necessarily values the simplest of things for themselves because it has often had nothing else to work with. China's achievement of a reasonable life for its people has been extraordinary, but comforts – and diet – are not what they are for many in the West, who would find on the menu a lot less meat and a great deal more of things like cabbage and turnip than they are used to. There is a good deal of starch in the daily diet, with such things as steamed breads, pancakes, rice and *congee* (rice porridge): noodle shops are popular, and dumplings are the Chinese hamburger – eaten in the streets, at the railway stations, in the factories. There is an element of competition in eating them – people boast how many, like the Germans. They may be *baozi*, fried; or *jiaozi*, steamed. Either way, they are a good recipe to take from a People's Republic.

Meat chopped in a food processor will have a rather more authentic texture than minced meat, since the original method is to chop the filling ingredients exceedingly finely with a cleaver. The original recipe used pork which was at least a quarter fat. Use other vegetables, other meats, additional flavourings and varying proportions as you choose. Shrimp, cucumber and pork is another combination.

# MEAT AND CABBAGE DUMPLINGS
## (Jiaozi)
NORTHERN CHINA

MAKES AT LEAST 4 DOZEN SMALL DUMPLINGS

| |
|---|
| 450 g (1 lb) plain flour (preferably strong flour) |
| About 275 ml ($\frac{1}{2}$ pint) water |
| 225 g ($\frac{1}{2}$ lb) pork or other meat, finely minced |
| 3 slices of fresh ginger, finely minced |
| 3 spring onions, finely chopped |
| 3 tablespoons soy sauce |
| 3 tablespoons wine (rice wine or dry sherry) |
| 3 teaspoons sesame oil |
| 1 teaspoon salt |
| Up to 1 teaspoon monosodium glutamate, if you insist |
| 100 g ($\frac{1}{4}$ lb) Chinese leaves or cabbage, spinach, Pak Choi, finely chopped |

PREPARATION: Make a fairly firm flour and water dough, kneading well, and set aside to rest for half an hour. Put a large pan of water on to boil.

Mix the meat and the other stuffing ingredients and flavourings except the Chinese leaves and stir a little cold water into it until you have a slurry like thick porridge. Add the Chinese leaves.

Knead the dough again, roll into a sausage about 2·5 cm (1 inch) thick and pull off pieces to make into balls. Flatten the balls and roll them out into discs whose edge is thinner than the middle. Put some filling on each piece of dough, fold over into a half-moon shape and crimp the edges attractively.

When the cooking water is boiling, add the dumplings. They are done when they rise to the top (and a sprinkle of cold water will take any rubbish that has risen with them back to the bottom). Serve with such seasonings as flavoured oil or vinegar, soy sauce or a chilli or sweet and sour sauce.

Two thousand years before Mao, the philosopher Mencius gave his advice on how to rule: 'For each family, five acres of orchard planted with mulberry trees … Let them have chickens, pigs, dogs and swine to breed … Give each family a hundred acres for its crops … One whose subjects wear silk and eat flesh when they are old, within whose frontiers the common people are never famished, never cold, cannot fail to become a True King.'

Many an emperor has been found wanting by much lower standards than this. And periodic revolution has always been part of the Chinese way of life. Where we had the divine right of kings (a god-given licence to take rights away from everybody else), the Chinese emperors ruled under the mandate of heaven: as long as they ruled tolerably, the dynasty survived. When they alienated the people and caused rebellions, the goodwill of the gods was withdrawn along with that of their subjects.

The long line of Chinese dynasties actually ended at the start of our century, when the formidably self-centred Empress Dowager was deposed, after a career which had included treating herself to a new Summer Palace on the money set aside to build a Chinese navy. The Palace of the Jade Waves came in useful as a prison for her own son, the Emperor, after he had shown disquieting tendencies towards social reform: she kept him locked up there for ten years. Today, the palace is even more useful as a tourist attraction and symbol of the decadence of the Empire – an excellent opportunity to point out the sins and indulgences of the court, down to how the Empress ordered an extravagant variety of porridges for breakfast. Which does indeed serve her right. If her bossy spirit could only see it, probably the worst thing of all would be the spectacle of Western tourist barbarians having their pictures taken grinning and giggling in the costumes of the imperial court.

The Summer Palace stands on a wooded hillside overlooking the lake fed by the waters of the Jade Spring, diverted in the Yuan dynasty – for though this palace is nineteenth century, its predecessors go back to the twelfth century. Its Long Corridor follows the shoreline for almost half a mile of trellised arcades, paintings of the seasons and conscientiously perfect views across the lake. It leads past the Palace that Dispels Clouds, built as a place of celebration for the Empress's birthdays; and Tingli Guan, the Hall in which to Listen to Golden Orioles, formerly a theatre. Tingli Guan is now a restaurant, but still has more drama about it sometimes than many of us would like.

It is a place of soft, bright carpets and venerable plush and mahogany chairs; and they still make some of the dishes served up at the Banquet of Long Life, the Empress's birthday dinner. Dragon and Phoenix Presenting Auspiciousness was apparently a favourite – a gaudy and gigantic pictorial hors-d'œuvre of a large green-and-white dragon and a plump bird arguing at each other, but impeded by the presence of a jade pearl and a golden ring in their respective mouths.

And – this is the touch of unpleasant drama – they still eat live fish, thanks to the kitchen techniques known as Three Quicknesses and One Skilfulness – which basically employ the same skill and quicknesses as those for which our own medieval hangmen were celebrated.

An apparently ordinary family – young executive father, mother in Western-style fashions, little boy, beaming old grandmother (obviously out for her own birthday banquet on Longevity Hill, just like the Empress) – go to a pool with their waitress, and choose a great, wriggling carp.

It goes to the kitchen – carp live out of water longer than most other fish – and is scaled and gutted like lightning. Slices are cut diagonally into its body from gills to tail and it is held by the head with a napkin and its body plunged into boiling oil for thirty seconds or so. By the time it has been sauced and sent to table, its gills are still moving, its front fins waving and its mouth opening. Father and mother clap; grandmother beams even more; and the little boy gives it a little cup of rice wine to drink. When the alcohol gets into its mouth, it gapes and pants even more, and everybody laughs. Then they set to it with the chopsticks and when its body is eaten its mouth still moves, a little.

It is not the only such dish in the history of Chinese food. On the other hand, there was also a man who would water his dish of rice with dew from the flowers, and leave it covered for a while just before serving.

The cooking is like China itself, this country which has more beliefs and minority races than there are dishes on a table at a banquet. It is inclusive rather than exclusive; it remembers rather than forgets; and tolerates all kinds of co-existence – philosophy, pretension, poetry, vulgarity, extravagance, poverty, puritanism, cruelty.

# SUZHOU, JIANGSU PROVINCE

*'Heaven above: below, Suzhou and Hangzhou.'* A monk of the Song Dynasty

Suzhou (Soochow) is an hour and a half by train from Shanghai in the intensively farmed Jiangsu (Yangtse) Delta, a country of canals and ditches. The water continues within the town, so that it is sometimes called the Venice of the East, but you could just as well call it the Chinese Pisa, since it also has a leaning pagoda, Cloud Rock Temple on Tiger Hill. It is a town for strolling through, over streams crossed by thousands of little bridges, among old white houses, along leafy streets of plane trees. In the past there were tea-houses with girls and music (by legend, Suzhou women are particularly beautiful). Today there is one of the world's great little confectioners, a small shop with a hundred different recipes for sweets and pastries, with half that number in the window as the standard display. Generally, Chinese cakes are not distinguished, being rather solid, but Suzhou cakes are famous. They vary in flavour from sticky sweet to something on the way to being savoury, are often rice-based and use only natural flavour and colouring – with nuts, juices, egg, bean and preserved fruits. Four Coloured Delicacies, for instance, are rice flour shells enclosing a filling and made in the forms of animals, fruit and vegetables – miniature purple aubergines, red and yellow pears, golden corncobs, red radishes. They were first made during the Ming dynasty, like the vases.

The decoration taught at the Suzhou Cooking School is part of an artistic tradition which also includes the making of fine mahogany furniture and silk production and embroidery ranging from factory goods to the prestigious showpieces of the Embroidery Institute. There is screen-painting, there is food-painting – both survivals of courtly life in the age of the common man; and both still thought to be worth the prodigality of skill and labour that goes into them.

Suzhou is a cultivated town in every sense. Its tradition of scholarship brought it great success in the Imperial Examinations, the bureaucratic ritual through which a student passed to a life of power or which held him back in obscurity. Today, there is a school in the Twin Pagodas which, with the Ink Pagoda, stood by the old examination hall.

Eager, the students went out into the world; disillusioned, they returned to seek peace in gardens made with all the poetry and art of which they were capable. The Garden of the Humble Administrator is Ming (created just about the time when Henry VIII was discovering girls), and contains a Hall of Distant Fragrance, a Rainbow Bridge and a Pavilion of Clarity and Magnificence. (The mandarin himself, Wang Xiachen, had been kicked downstairs by his own bureaucracy. Perhaps this made him humble, or perhaps he was humble before, and this was why he was demoted, a humble administrator being a contradiction in terms.)

In the Tarrying Garden are the Hall of the Immortals of the Five Peaks and the Returning to My Reading Place Pavilion; in the Lion Grove Garden, the Pavilion of Genuine Delight; in the Garden of the Master of the Nets, the Hall for Staying Spring; in the West Garden, the Pond in which to Set Free the Captive Fish; on Tiger Hill, the Third Spring under Heaven – a 1400-year-old well whose water is famous (and was classically rated Number 3 in the world) for the making of jasmine tea, which is much grown nearby.

Suzhou had a hundred such gardens – the first of them built before the Norman Conquest (which was 1500 years after the first founding of the city). The search for a poetic quality in life was repeated in eating. Suzhou cuisine became noted for an ultra-refinement which turned the chef into the culinary counterpart of those people who make china shepherdesses. The maintenance of 'face' was, and is, important in China: but there was so much face in Suzhou cooking that you wonder where the body went.

The Vegetarian Feast presented at the Deyuelou Restaurant, Suzhou, is not simple, economical – or even vegetarian.

The Peacock Hors-d'œuvre is scarcely less spectacular than the bird it represents. There are eight side-dishes, whose arrangement merely has to be exquisite, and the centrepiece – an imitation peacock with its tail and wings spread. The only concession to making life easier for the chef is that at least the bird is sitting down. The neck and head are made out of beancurd sheets steamed on a form; the substance of the body is mashed potato with slices of chicken, mushroom and onion – also steamed; and the wings and tail are exceedingly elaborate decoration with slices of meat for most of the wings and vegetables for the tail. The recipe calls for a boiled chicken, a boiled duck, boiled ham, dried Chinese mushrooms, potatoes, sheets of beancurd, red cherries, fresh bamboo shoots, cloves of garlic, cooked lettuce roots, onion, and condiments, not to mention obsessional patience and artistic ability.

Cream-dressed beancurd is a comparatively simple dish, being plain white with dark mushrooms, and having only a flower made with a mushroom stem and a rosette of carrot as decoration ('to resemble plum blossom bursting in snow'). For those sceptical about beancurd, this is a rather bland dish: substituting yogurt for cream might make it a little less so, but adequate initial seasoning is important.

# CREAM-DRESSED BEANCURD WITH MUSHROOM
## DEYUELOU RESTAURANT, SUZHOU, JIANGSU PROVINCE
### IN COMBINATION WITH OTHER DISHES, ENOUGH FOR 4 PEOPLE

| |
|---|
| 350 g (12 oz) beancurd rubbed through a sieve |
| 125 ml (4 fl oz) double cream |
| Salt and white pepper |
| About 2 teaspoons lemon juice |
| Soy sauce |
| Sesame oil |
| 50 g (2 oz) dried Chinese mushrooms, soaked and drained |
| Cornflour for flouring and thickening |
| About 4 tablespoons groundnut oil |
| About 1 glass wine (rice wine, spirit or sherry) |
| *Garnish* (optional) |
| 1 small carrot |

PREPARATION: Mix the beancurd with the cream, seasoning to taste with salt, white pepper and lemon juice and about 1 teaspoon of soy sauce and 2 teaspoons of sesame oil. Use scissors to cut the mushroom caps into strips about the size of thick onion rings. Dip these in cornflour, deep-fry them until they are crisping and then toss them over heat in 2 tablespoons of soy sauce with the same amount of cornflour-and-water mixture and 1 tablespoon of sesame oil. Check seasoning and set on one side to marinate: they should emerge dark-coloured to contrast with the white beancurd.

Heat the groundnut oil very hot in a wok or frying pan. Toss in the wine to flame and, immediately afterwards, the beancurd mixture: sauté vigorously for about 5 minutes.

Put out the beancurd on the serving dish, and decorate with the mushrooms (and carrot, if you feel inclined).

The Vegetarian Feast also included such humble fare as Eight Coloured Dishes, Fried Shrimps within a Lantern, Three Delicacies of Bright Moon, Pigeon and Pine, Deep-fried Duck, Braised Shark's Fin with Butterfly Pattern, Mandarin Duck Soup with Water Shield and Sautéed Chinese 'Perch' with Eight Ingredients.

Unlike the duck (which was duck), the 'perch' really was vegetarian – being mashed potato mounted on a sheet of beancurd with a filling in its middle. Again, the style was bland, the nearest approach to flavour in the stuffing being smoked beancurd. Most of the taste was provided by the sweet and sour sauce (which here is not the original Suzhou sauce but an invented recipe). It is a dish to use as a basis for improvisation rather than one to reproduce; and I would recommend another stuffing (even real fish?), though I give the original. The quantities may seem small, but they are more than ample for the space available, given the low tensile strength of mashed potato.

Beancurd sheets are very brittle when dry, turn leathery when wet, taste of little but a slight sourness, and erupt interestingly in hot oil (I made some very un-Chinese cheese puffs with mine by wrapping up pieces of Roquefort), and are potentially useful as a foundation for set-piece dishes. Since a free-standing mashed potato sculpture is always in considerable danger of falling apart, it is a good idea to use about four sheets as the basis for the 'perch', brushed with beaten egg to keep them together.

# SAUTÉED CHINESE 'PERCH' WITH EIGHT INGREDIENTS

## DEYUELOU RESTAURANT, SUZHOU, JIANGSU PROVINCE

IN COMBINATION WITH OTHER DISHES, ENOUGH FOR 4 PEOPLE

| |
|---|
| 4 beancurd sheets |
| 1 beaten egg |
| 6 to 8 potatoes, boiled and stiffly mashed (seasoned with salt and pepper) |
| 2 dried Chinese mushrooms, soaked and drained |
| 8 × 5 cm (2 inch) strips of bamboo shoot |
| Groundnut oil for deep-frying |
| *Filling* |
| 1 tablespoon smoked (or plain) beancurd, finely chopped |
| 4 dried Chinese mushrooms, soaked and finely chopped |
| 1 tablespoon bamboo shoots, finely chopped |
| 1 tablespoon young broad beans, skinned and finely chopped |
| 1 tablespoon bean sprouts, finely chopped |
| 1 teaspoon soy sauce |
| 1 teaspoon seasame oil |
| $\frac{1}{2}$ teaspoon flour |
| *Sauce* |
| 2 tablespoons Hoi Sin sauce |
| 1 tablespoon soy sauce |
| 1 tablespoon sesame oil |
| 2 tablespoons lemon juice |
| 2 tablespoons water |

PREPARATION: Cook the filling ingredients gently together for about 5 minutes in a covered pan. Wet the beancurd sheets and smooth them on to the chopping board, brushing with beaten egg to stick them together. Make the shape of a fish in mashed potato, leaving a hole in the abdomen for the filling. Line the bottom of the hole with potato, add the filling and cover with potato. Decorate with a mushroom eye and gills and slices of bamboo for fins. Scratch a scale pattern with a knife. Trim off the excess beancurd sheet.

Heat a well-supported wok of oil very hot. Carefully slide in the 'fish' and deep-fry it until it is golden brown, basting any parts that protrude above the surface. Mix the sauce ingredients and heat. Pour over the 'fish' and serve.

All cuisines steer their own course between excess and simplicity, and in China the voyage has been long under way. In the second century BC they were marinating beef in wine and making meatballs: in the sixth century BC, Confucius was being a fusspot at dinner-time. (Great thinkers are not normally the best of people to cook for, since in their abstraction they are liable to let their camel hump get cold; but Confucius was a real pain about food. 'It was not properly cooked – he would not eat it. It was not in season – he would not eat it. It was not cut correctly – he would not eat it. It was not served with its proper sauce – he would not eat it then, either.') What Confucius said for himself was that everyone eats and drinks: but few people have taste.

Nevertheless, Chinese cuisine is discriminating: with all the excesses of the gastronomes over two millennia, simplicity and food that was true to itself remained an ideal – even if sometimes a forgotten one. There is even a phrase for it which translates, more or less, as 'Flavour is truth, truth flavour ...' This is *hsien*, only one word in a precise cooking vocabulary. *Hsiang* is the essential fragrance of a food; *nung*, concentrated flavour; *yu-er-pu-ni*, the savour of fat. The basic textures are: *tsuei*, crisp and crunchy; *nun*, tender with resilience; *ruan*, a melting softness. The place where they understand this language best is in the south – in Guangdong (Canton) province and Hong Kong.

# HONG KONG

# HONG KONG AND ITS CANTONESE COOKERY

*'The test of the stew lies in what the chopstick brings to the surface.'* Ernest Bramah, *Kai Lung Beneath the Mulberry Tree*

Hong Kong, 'the fragrant harbour on the Pearl river', teems in tower blocks, in shanties, in the harbour junks and sampans. Hong Kong is a market-place in which everything is for sale, and always was: having become the commercial successor to Canton when British traders were excluded from the mainland because they trafficked so hugely in opium. From both West and East people came to Hong Kong to make money. The island was like the waist of an hour-glass, where all grains of sand must pass, no matter in which direction they are going, and rub up against each other in the process. People also came to escape, as they had before. The Hakka in the New Territories were refugees in the fifteenth century – but their name still means 'guest people'. Boat people, refugees from the Red Guard, whoever fled successfully created a human soup that boils over all the parts of waterfront, city, island and mountain where a human foot can get a toehold – and a number of places where it can't.

It is no ordinary soup. Not only had Canton been a city of middlemen accustomed to profit from the toings-and-froings between ancient China and the go-getting West: its people had long had a reputation for adventurousness, energy and ingenuity. The combination of the Chinese will to survive with a capitalist free-for-all is formidable – exhilarating, cruel, poetic, affectionate, unsentimental. Hong Kong has the same sort of hustle and jostle as Victorian London is said to have had; and the same sort of casualty rate in social values. People are kind to each other at home: out in the city, they do business (unless, of course, being kind to strangers is their business) and they eat – at stalls, at restaurants and at the teahouses, where breakfast or lunch is *dim-sum.*

*Dim-sum*, Delights of the Heart, are sometimes more than food: they are an entertainment. A *dim-sum* restaurant can be the size of a cinema, seating not hundreds but thousands, with the food not ordered individually but peddled by girls with trolleys and trays, like the ice cream girl at the pictures or the theatre. (To complete the resemblance, *dim-sum* chefs can be stars, dashing from one restaurant to another to give a performance of their speciality, like Marie Lloyd with her hansom cab at the stage door.)

*Dim-sum* include such dishes as delicate dumplings with various fillings, prawns steamed in thin leaves of pastry, pork buns, chicken wrapped with beancurd. There are sweet *dim-sum*, too – but the basic principle of most of the dishes is to package.

The best-known parcel of all is the spring roll; and the spring roll is an object lesson in the harmonious contrast of tastes and textures. A spring roll wrapper is *mille-feuille* without the other 999 layers. In Britain, you can buy them in Chinese shops and adventurous delicatessens – even in some supermarkets. They are about twice the size of *wuntun* skins. The thing to watch is to keep them flexible by making sure they do not dry out. Wrap them well in the refrigerator or freezer, and cover them with a damp cloth when they are out in the kitchen. The filling needs something crisp (bean sprouts, bamboo shoots, water chestnuts, celery, sweet peppers) with a more solid flavour (meat, prawn, mushroom): keeping those two qualities in mind, you can vary the dish as you like.

# SPRING ROLLS
## A HONG KONG FAMILY
### IN COMBINATION WITH OTHER DISHES, ENOUGH FOR 4 PEOPLE

| |
|---|
| **50 g (2 oz) Chinese mushrooms** |
| **50 g (2 oz) bamboo shoots** |
| **1 egg, beaten** |
| **4 spring onions** |
| **Light oil, such as groundnut oil, for frying** |
| **225 g (8 oz) pork (preferably a lean cut, such as fillet), shredded** |
| **100 g (4 oz) bean sprouts** |
| **8 spring roll wrappers** |
| **Cornflour and water paste or a little more beaten egg** |
| *Marinade* |
| **Sesame oil** |
| **Light soy sauce** |
| **Cornflour** |
| **Sugar** |

PREPARATION: Marinate the pork (don't drown it) in sesame oil and soy sauce with some cornflour and a little sugar. Soak the mushrooms in water for about half an hour. If the bamboo shoots are fresh, blanch them for a minute to take off their bitterness. Make a thin omelette and shred it (quicker if you fold it several times). Cut the mushrooms into small pieces, trimming the stalks if necessary. Cut the onions into 4 cm (1½ inch) lengths and cut the lengths into strips. Sliver the bamboo shoots.

Sauté the mushrooms and bamboo shoots in a little oil in a wok or frying pan, then add the pork and stir-fry. Add the remaining marinade (there should not be too much) and, when the meat is almost done, toss in the onion, shredded omelette and beansprouts and mix well. Transfer the mixture to a bowl and let it cool, uncovered.

Fold the wrappers round the filling, sealing the edges with cornflour and water, or with beaten egg. (For the method of folding, think of the wrapper, round or square, as a face: put filling on the eyes and fold the forehead over it; bring in the ears and fold them over the sides of the face; roll the resultant packet up in the chin.)

Deep-fry the spring rolls. If you are deep-frying in a wok, make sure it is properly supported. Heat the oil for deep-frying to a moderately high temperature (too low makes them soggy, too high burns them). It should be short of smoking, about 180°C (350°F) – a piece of spring onion thrown into it will bubble and move about. Cook until golden brown.

~~ • ~~

You can get any kind of Chinese food in Hong Kong, but its local cuisine, Cantonese, is the one which has brought Chinese food to the West. It is lighter and fresher than northern Chinese food, and the capitalist culture and prosperous tourism and commerce of Hong Kong allow it to blossom, and sometimes to be extravagant. Contact with the West has also made it a much better communicated cuisine than other Chinese styles.

The traditional overcrowding has intensified the Chinese liking for eating in restaurants; and even today – despite all the housing programmes – the sort of ordinary people who do not live in shacks may find it difficult to feed and accommodate friends at home. As in France, such an eating-out culture makes for good restaurants; and Cantonese cooking has the same sort of professional quality as the French – a combination of being down-to-earth in what you do, yet being capable of unerring flights of subtlety. The result is a cooking style which respects ingredients, and produces delicious results; but which is also practical, sometimes to the point of being easy – and which can be cheap. Like all non-ceremonial Chinese cooking, it depends on something filling – rice, noodles and so on – in combination with more elaborate, often made-up, dishes in which the expensive ingredients are likely to be in quite small quantities. Freshness is crucial. Hong Kong abounds in markets and stalls, and a cook may take the trouble to shop twice a day in the expectation that something new may have come in.

The recipes are well judged and clever: so it is a great pity to shower them with monosodium glutamate, as is often done in Western Chinese restaurants (even apart from the fact that heavy doses of the raw chemical make some people ill). Beware, too, of excessive five-spice powder, and of all over-seasoning. For once white pepper is to be preferred to black, but, as always, it should be freshly ground.

Stir-frying is a common cooking method. The food is tossed in a light oil, such as groundnut oil, in a hot wok, which may be covered to steam the food a little as well: but the general principle – especially for vegetables – is minimal cooking with fairly minimal moisture.

The recipe for Lettuce Rolls with Prawns is a perfect example of how natural flavours are brought out by the cooking method and the combination of ingredients. If you don't have a steamer you can improvise a steaming platform by arranging chopsticks across the top of a wok. If your fishmonger only has cooked prawns they will not crush like the raw ones and form a paste, but you can wrap them up whole as a second-best. Or use fish, or other things – it is such an easy and pretty idea that there is some danger of becoming obsessed with wrapping things in lettuce leaves. The leaves themselves need to be rather large – a Webb's-type lettuce is best.

# LETTUCE ROLLS WITH PRAWNS
### A HONG KONG FAMILY
### IN COMBINATION WITH OTHER DISHES, ENOUGH FOR 4 PEOPLE

| |
|---|
| **450 g (1 lb) raw prawns, peeled and de-veined** |
| **Salt and pepper** |
| **1 large-leaved lettuce** |
| **1 tablespoon cornflour** |
| **125 ml (4 fl oz) water** |
| **2 tablespoons oyster sauce** |

PREPARATION: Rub the prawns with salt, wash them and dry them thoroughly, then crush them with the blade of a cleaver or heavy knife. Put them in a bowl, season lightly with salt and pepper and stir until they are all bound together in a paste. Boil the lettuce leaves in salted water for a minute or so until they are limp enough to fold into a parcel. Dry them and wrap them round a filling of prawn paste, making the same folds as for spring rolls (page 156). Steam the rolls for 10 minutes. Mix the cornflour and water, add the oyster sauce and cook for one minute before pouring the sauce over the rolls.

The pork spare ribs *en papillote* are marinated for flavour, and the paper keeps the flavour in, as well as the protecting the meat from the hot oil. The method can also be used for other meats, such as chicken and beef. Kitchen foil is easy to screw up into a packet if you are going to unwrap the ribs before they go to table, but serving them in the paper is more elegant and more fun. They can be a little fiddly to undo, though – use a stout waxed paper like Bakewell paper in preference to ordinary greaseproof.

# SPARE RIBS IN PAPER

## HONG KONG

### IN COMBINATION WITH OTHER DISHES, ENOUGH FOR 4 PEOPLE

| |
|---|
| **450 g (1 lb) pork spare ribs, chopped into sections about 4 cm (1½ inches) long** |
| **Groundnut oil for deep-frying** |
| *Marinade* |
| **1 tablespoon vinegar** |
| **1 tablespoon rice wine or sherry** |
| **1 tablespoon light soy sauce** |
| **½ tablespoon sesame oil** |
| **1 spring onion, finely chopped** |
| **1 clove garlic, finely chopped** |
| **4 slices ginger, finely chopped** |
| **2 tablespoons cornflour** |
| **Pinch of sugar** |
| **And you'll need some greaseproof paper, cut into 10 cm (4 inch) squares** |

PREPARATION: Mix the marinade ingredients, cover the spare ribs with the marinade and leave at least 1 hour and preferably overnight.

Give the ribs a last toss in the marinade and wrap them up in paper packets. Put a rib near one corner of the paper, fold the corner over it, and roll the rib and paper over once. Fold both sides over the middle. Roll the rib over again and tuck the remaining corner into the pocket between the folds of paper underneath.

If you are deep-frying in a wok, make sure it is properly supported. Deep-fry the packets in moderately hot oil until the spare ribs are brown. Drain on kitchen paper, and slit each packet with a razor-blade or scissors before serving.

Beggar's Chicken (unplucked chicken baked in mud), Drunken Chicken (the Chinese *coq au vin*): there are hundreds of chicken dishes. My Lord's Smoked Chicken finds yet another use for the wok — as a smoke-house: a cooked chicken is put on a rack with some green (or other exotic) tea, cassia buds, flour and sugar on a piece of foil at the bottom, and the wok is covered and kept hot for half an hour.

The recipe for sautéed diced chicken is straightforward and well adapted to Western taste: the cashews (which should be fresh) are a perfect complement in flavour and texture to the chicken, which is sealed with a transparent layer of cornflour and egg white. Hoi Sin sauce is sometimes called a barbecue sauce, though it is more subtle and less tangy. Here it is just a quick means of adding a Chinese flavour. It is quite easily available.

# DICED CHICKEN SAUTÉED WITH SWEET PEPPERS AND CASHEW NUTS
### A HONG KONG FAMILY
### IN COMBINATION WITH OTHER DISHES, ENOUGH FOR 4 PEOPLE

| |
|---|
| 175 g (6 oz) chicken breast, skinned and cut into 1 cm (½ inch) dice |
| 1 tablespoon cornflour |
| 1 teaspoon salt |
| ½ teaspoon sugar |
| 1 egg white |
| Groundnut oil for deep-frying and stir-frying |
| 100 g (4 oz) fresh cashew nuts (almonds, walnuts, or even peanuts can be substituted) |
| 1 cm (½ inch) length of fresh ginger, peeled and sliced |
| 3 spring onions, cut into 5 cm (2 inch) lengths |
| ½ a green and ½ a red pepper, chopped |
| 1 tablespoon Hoi Sin sauce |

PREPARATION: Mix the diced chicken with the cornflour, salt, sugar and egg white, turning it well. If you are going to deep-fry in a wok, make sure it is properly supported. Heat the oil to 180°C (350°F) — a piece of onion dropped in should sizzle and move about in it. Deep-fry the chicken until it is no longer pink, and drain on kitchen paper. Deep-fry the cashew nuts to a rich golden brown and drain on kitchen paper. Pour away the deep-frying oil.

Stir-fry the ginger slices with the onions and the red and green peppers in a little fresh oil. After a minute or so mix in the chicken and cook till everything is hot. Stir in the nuts and the Hoi Sin sauce.

~ • ~

Chinese stock is not a grand free-for-all of meat and pot herbs, as in the West. The essential flavour of the meat is preserved by restricting additions to a few slices of ginger and perhaps a spring onion or two.

As this simple crab soup treats the stock and the crab meat separately, it is not important to have all the shelly bits to boil down to add flavour, so frozen or tinned crab is a possible substitute (though of course it is never the real thing), and other shellfish can be used instead.

# SOUP WITH CRAB MEAT AND EGG FOO YUNG

## A HONG KONG FAMILY

### ENOUGH FOR 4 PEOPLE

| |
|---|
| **1 litre (1¾ pints) chicken or veal stock** |
| **Salt and pepper** |
| **3 heaped tablespoons cornflour, blended with 4 tablespoons cold water** |
| **1 crab, cooked, meat extracted** |
| **1 egg, beaten** |

PREPARATION: Heat the stock, salting and peppering it. Stir the cornflour blend into the boiling stock, continuing to stir until the soup thickens. Add the crab meat. Bring the soup to a brisk boil and pour it into the beaten egg in a thin stream, stirring vigorously with chopsticks.

The Chinese are fanatical about the freshness of fish. In the seafood restaurants, some of which are themselves aquatic and vary from shanties on sampans to floating fish-palaces, tanks of live creatures await an abrupt end, followed by almost as rapid cooking. A crab will be picked out, snapping claws and all, and taken apart with a cleaver with just a quick preliminary chop from the underside between the eyes. The shell is levered off, its ingrowing edges trimmed off with the cleaver (cutting parallel with the shell), and the tail flap removed; the mouth and stomach and the fibrous white 'dead men's fingers' are taken out; the claws are chopped at the joints and broken with the flat of the blade; and the legs are well trimmed back but left attached to sections of the body.

# FRIED CRAB WITH SPRING ONIONS AND GINGER

A HONG KONG FAMILY

ENOUGH FOR 2 PEOPLE

| |
|---|
| **Groundnut oil for deep-frying and stir-frying** |
| **1 crab, cooked, meat cut up and dusted with cornflour** |
| **2·5 cm (1 inch) length of ginger, sliced** |
| **6 spring onions, cut into 5 cm (2 inch) lengths** |
| **1 or more cloves of garlic, minced** |
| **2 teaspoons cornflour, blended with 1 tablespoon cold water** |
| **Salt and pepper** |
| **Sugar** |
| **Oyster sauce (optional)** |

It you are using a wok for frying, make sure it is properly supported and stable. Fill the wok or other deep pan half-full of oil and heat it to quite hot. Throw the pieces of crab into the hot oil and deep-fry them very briefly, just enough to seal them. Take them out and drain them well on kitchen paper. Empty out the deep-frying oil.

Sauté the ginger, onions and minced garlic in fresh oil. Toss the crab with the flavourings, cover and cook for 5 minutes. Add the cornflour over heat, stirring till the mixture thickens. Season with salt, pepper, a little sugar and – if you like – oyster sauce.

~~ • ~~

Onion and ginger are the inveterate companions of Hong Kong seafood of all kinds, including the hefty local oysters. These oysters were originally cultivated for the making of oyster sauce – which I am inclined to describe as 'the Marmite of the ocean'. It is much less concentrated than Marmite, though. Oyster sauce has a subtle flavour which adds a something to meat cooking, in particular.

The oyster himself is an obstinate beast. He spends his life a-swim in seawater; and when he is cooked he gives off so much liquid that he is soon a-swim again. The effect is minimised here by cooking the oysters in three brief stages, draining them in between. Oysters need little cooking, and toughen if they get too much: in general, three or four minutes' simmering will poach an oyster – the edges curl when they are done. (Their liquor is not used in this recipe, but it is always worth saving for something else.) The cornflour treatment specified in the recipe is partly to help clean the oysters and partly to improve the texture. An alternative way of treating them is to rub them with salt, leave them for a few moments, then rinse.

The ginger wine is not British Christmas ginger wine, but fresh ginger blended with rice wine or sherry and strained through a cloth — a useful concoction like mild sherry peppers (see p. 95). It is very easy to make in an electric blender.

# SAUTÉED OYSTERS WITH SPRING ONIONS AND GINGER
## A HONG KONG FISH RESTAURANT
### IN COMBINATION WITH OTHER DISHES, ENOUGH FOR 4 PEOPLE

| |
|---|
| 8 oysters, shelled |
| 3 or 4 tablespoons groundnut oil |
| 8 spring onions, cut into 5 cm (2 inch) lengths |
| 2·5 cm (1 inch) length fresh ginger, sliced |
| 125 ml (4 fl oz) chicken or veal stock |
| Salt and pepper |
| Sugar |
| Oyster sauce |
| Ginger wine |
| 2 teaspoons cornflour blended with 1 tablespoon cold water, and extra cornflour for cleaning the oysters |

PREPARATION: Rub the oysters with the cornflour to clean off grit and débris. Boil enough water to cover the oysters in the bottom of a wok or a pan, toss in the oysters and leave them for a few seconds. Drain them.

Shallow-fry the oysters in 2 or 3 tablespoons of oil, adding the onions and ginger. Cook uncovered and not too fiercely for 1 or 2 minutes, until they are three-quarters done. Drain.

Sauté the oysters (with the onions and ginger) in 1 tablespoon of oil. Almost at once, add the stock, salt, pepper, a sprinkle of sugar and oyster sauce. Cook for about a minute, then add a splash of ginger wine. Stir in the cornflour and water to thicken the sauce.

Despite voracious fishing, there is a watery cornucopia of fish in Hong Kong, with names which sound as if the spirit of Chinese poetry has run down into the sea: red snapper, wave sea bream, conger pike, golden thread, lizard fish, Macao sole. Mackerel, bonito, sharks and manta rays come in August and

September; the yellow croaker (otherwise known as the golden flower or the jewfish) arrives in October and November. (They really do croak – skilled fishermen listen for them with an ear pressed to the bottom of the boat.)

Carp are reared in the ponds of the New Territories (which is where the islands get the food that does not come downriver from China herself), with ducks for another part of the banquet swimming ignorantly on the surface. The flesh is sometimes said to taste muddy, so that the fish needs extra washing and soaking in a light wash of vinegar, but not all carp are bottom feeders like the mud carp and common carp. The grass carp feeds at every level and the big-head carp and silver carp feed at the top of the pond.

One Suzhou recipe for carp poaches the fish in a broth of mutton, wine and onion in which pieces of the fish are then served. But the Cantonese gourmet favours the relative simplicity of steaming. You can improvise a steaming platform across a wok, in the same way as for Lettuce Rolls (see page 158). Once again, there is no escaping ginger and spring onions – but this time the cooked onions are not eaten. They are also there to influence the flavour, but their main purpose is to stop the fish sticking to the plate and allow the steam to pass underneath. Raw onions are used for garnish. The Cantonese gourmets eat the brains, which, along with the skin, are particularly esteemed.

# STEAMED FISH

### A HONG KONG FISH RESTAURANT

### ENOUGH FOR 2 PEOPLE

| |
|---|
| 1 whole carp or other fish of about 750 g (1¾ lb) |
| 10 spring onions |
| 100 g (¼ lb) Chinese preserved ham (or cured raw ham, such as Parma ham), sliced |
| 4 mushrooms, sliced |
| 4 cm (1½ inch) length of fresh ginger, sliced |
| 125 ml (4 fl oz) oil |
| Soy sauce |
| *Garnish* |
| A sprig of parsley |

PREPARATION: Heat the steamer. Put ice cubes in a bowl of water. Scale, clean and dry the fish. Make onion brushes for the garnish by cutting a cross down either end of a 10 cm (4 inch) length of spring onion for about 4 cm (1½ inches). Do this to 6 or 7 of the spring onions. Put them in iced water – the ends will curl up and delight those who admire such things.

Put the fish on its serving dish resting on 3 or 4 spring onion stalks. Lay alternate and overlapping slices of ham, mushrooms and ginger along the length of the fish. Steam at full blast for about 10 minutes for a fat fish, 8 minutes for a flat fish. Meanwhile, heat the oil just short of smoking point.

Take out the plate, dry the moisture from it and discard the spring onions. Pour the hot oil all over the skin, and pour soy sauce either side of the fish, on the oil. Garnish with onion brushes and parsley.

Onion brushes are quite everyday, but carved fruit and vegetables – carrot butterflies, onion lilies (a horrid taste concept this, a carved onion with a glacé cherry at its centre), chains of cucumber rings and so on are a feature of the Chinese New Year's Day feast, the all-together family meal which is the equivalent of our Christmas dinner, even down to eating poultry.

Hong Kong may have one tendril in Whitehall and another in Threadneedle Street, but its roots are in the villages from which so many of its settlers came. Even with today's tower-blocks and boasted MTR (the underwater underground between Hong Kong island and Kowloon), the city keeps something of the quality of a peasant society, but running on people, commerce and sophistication instead of crops, animals and land. In particular, it keeps all the traditional Chinese festivals, which burst out brighter, livelier and noisier under pressure of population.

There are festival foods to go with them – *tahu yuen*, sweet balls of boiled rice flour at the Lantern Festival on the 15th day of the 1st moon, roast pig for Tam Kung the Weather God at the end of May, washing-up water on the birthday of Lord Buddha on the 8th day of the 4th moon – for they clean his statue and the water acquires virtue from the experience.

The Dragon Boat Festival summer at Midsummer commemorates the fourth-century patriot Chu Yuan, who was exiled for writing a poem about the decline of the kingdom, and drowned himself. The long, impossibly slender dragon boats, racing to the beat of drums, are also racing to his rescue. People eat sticky rice in bamboo leaves with sweet bean paste, minced pork, shellfish, duck egg or mixed vegetables. *Ch'un tze* are wrapped in bamboo leaves like the first offerings the river people made to the ghost of Chu; but the ghost appeared and said that the food thrown into the river was being eaten by a monster before he could get at it (like sparrows with milk bottles) and would they mind wrapping it up in iris leaves and tying it with five colours of silk? So they did, and the monster went hungry because he couldn't stand garnish.

At Chi'ing Ming festival – the Sweeping of the Graves – in early April, people burn money and consumer durables useful to a ghost, to the souls of their forefathers. Being Hong Kong, the money is imitation money and the durables are paper durables. This is a society close to the realities of existence, that at one time used to carry its fathers and mothers up the mountainside in their coffins and, with the greatest affection, leave them there until they died of exposure. Not even in the grave do they escape the overcrowding they have known in life, being dug up one Chi'ing Ming a few years on and their bones — cleaned and polished — placed in an urn less consuming of valuable space in the sort of nice, warm, south-facing grave that a discriminating spirit prefers. It is not that there is a lack of respect and affection for the elderly — this is a society which keeps its old people at home, rather than putting them in homes — but the Chinese are practical people, especially in Hong Kong. Even today, you find jade bracelets for sale which are cut in two — because they came off the wrist of a corpse.

So with fireworks and with lion dances (there are no lions in China, only lion dances) the festivals go round from New Year to New Year; when people pay their debts, clean the house to please the kitchen god and eat sweet foods so that he will sweet-talk the other gods on their behalf. They also eat Spiced Crispy Duck, a dish worthy of a special occasion: for, though Peking Duck is more famous, the Cantonese roasts are among the glories of Hong Kong — and this has to be considered an honorary roast.

Spiced crispy duck is the equivalent of the Christmas turkey: people are prepared to spend time on it; on and off, it takes about six or seven hours. The duck (or goose, as it sometimes is) is actually boiled: but after it has been anointed with a sweet-and-sour wash, air-dried and dripped over with hot oil to crisp and brown the skin, you would never know, to look at it. So this can be a roast for people who find themselves without an oven (to be called, I suppose, a wok-roast): but the honey-washing technique can be applied to any bird, given a few hours in advance of real roasting.

The star anise in the boiling is the spice that gives the penetrating flavour to five-spice powder (which is usually what gives the characteristic scent to Chinese restaurants and shops). It comes from a Chinese evergreen tree (not a Mediterranean umbellifer, like aniseed) and its seeds are arranged in a brown star: in non-Chinese cooking a single seed can be a hint, a whole star a firm statement. Five-spice powder can substitute.

# SPICED CRISPY DUCK

## A HONG KONG FAMILY

### IN COMBINATION WITH OTHER DISHES, ENOUGH FOR 4 TO 6 PEOPLE

| |
|---|
| 2·5 litres (4½ pints) water |
| 100 g (4 oz) salt |
| 2 tablespoons rice wine or sherry |
| 1 tablespoon star anise |
| 1 tablespoon peppercorns |
| 6 spring onions |
| 4 cm (1½ inch) length of fresh ginger, sliced |
| 1 duck |
| Groundnut oil for basting duck |
| *Honey wash* |
| A good ½ tablespoon honey |
| ½ tablespoon rice wine or sherry |
| 1 tablespoon vinegar |
| 1 tablespoon cornflour |
| You'll also need 6 or 7 hours minimum before serving and a willing helper (or at any rate a helper) for 15 minutes of the process |

PREPARATION: Bring the water to the boil with the salt, rice wine, star anise, peppercorns, whole spring onions and sliced ginger. Simmer for an hour, creating an exotic atmosphere in the kitchen. Add the duck for 25 minutes. Remove from the heat and leave it to steep for 30 minutes to an hour. Take it out and dry it with kitchen paper.

Cream the honey, wine and vinegar with the cornflour for the honey wash. Brush the duck all over with the wash and air-dry it overnight or for at least 3 or 4 hours, hanging in a draught or on a rack (a cooling fan speeds up the process, of course, if you are getting desperate; and a hair-dryer on full blast may constitute a new method of cookery in itself, apart from making your arm ache even before you get to the next stage).

Heat half a wok or large pan of groundnut oil to 180°C (350°F) — short of smoking. Get someone to hold the duck above the wok while you ladle the hot oil over it until the skin is very well browned, first on one side, then the other. This takes about 15 minutes in all. (Make sure helper, duck and wok are stable, and keep the oil up to temperature.) Serve the duck carved into bite-sized chunks.

The shiny rosy ducks and roast meats hanging in Chinatown windows all over the world are glazed with melted malt syrup after being roasted in a very hot oven, which will do a pork roast in 20 minutes. The pork (which needs to have some fat to keep it moist in the high temperatures) is cut in a strip so that the heat can cook the middle by the time the outside is seared, and marinated – usually with soy, sesame, ginger, sugar and salt, among other things.

## JAPAN

'There are the ones who watch and there are the fools who dance.
The ones who watch are fools to watch the fools who prance:
Since this is a universal rule, I'd rather be a dancing fool.'
Song of the dancers of the Awa Odori Festival, Tokushima

Mrs Beeton's Japanese Salad is a potato salad, with 12 anchovy fillets, onion, parsley, lettuce leaves, 18 cooked mussels, half a wineglassful of champagne, nutmeg and 3 medium-sized truffles.

If Mrs B. had provoked a Japanese with it, he would have called her a barbarian – possibly even a hairy barbarian, which would have been his pet expression for a foreigner. It would have been quite shocking. Fortunately, Mrs B. and the Japanese were strangers to each other: and strange into the bargain – not only Japan and Mrs Beeton, but Japan and the entire world. To most Westerners Japan is still strange. If the Orient is inscrutable, Japan is the most inscrutable bit of it. But just because it is so far off from our ideas it shows us very clearly how a nation's food is shaped by its geography, its history, its religion and even its art. For where, in the West, art interprets life, in Japan life is interpreted with art. The Japanese believe in beauty, even in food. They may also eat sliced bread and hamburgers, but the ideas of harmony, humility and tranquillity are as much at home in the Japanese kitchen as the idea of a chopping board.

The Japanese have an unusually large ration of an ability which is more common in ourselves than we care to notice: they are able to stuff their heads with all manner of quite contradictory ideas with hardly a twinge of a headache. So Japan is both chrysanthemums and transistors; fast food and fishing with cormorants. There is one ritual called the tea ceremony, and another in which they have to hire men to push the passengers on to the tube in the rush hour. The country is a blend of the most refined beauty and the most hideous mass modernity. On one hand the pace is frenetic – on the other, the place is timeless.

# KYOTO

*'The principle is always the same – to cause time to stop by making the hours elegant.'*
Kenichi Yoshida

A name like Heian-kyo, the Capital of Peace and Tranquillity, is asking for trouble, and most of what is now called Kyoto is not older than the seventeenth century, the city having been flattened in the civil wars that preceded the rule of the Tokugawa Shogunate. But Kyoto remained the Emperor's City for over a thousand years: even though the power in the land has often been elsewhere, and the capital moved to Edo (modern Tokyo) well over three centuries ago. To this day it is the place of coronation; and it was the sun of Japan's golden age, the Heian period, which produced the world's first novel, Murasaki Shikibu's *The Tale of Genji*, along with a courtly life-style of restrained elegance and great taste.

Looking at any Japanese city today is like composing a beautiful scene through the viewfinder of one of their remarkable cameras – it is necessary to shut the other eye. Kyoto has urban sprawl, industry, smog, office blocks and traffic jams. It also has silk, gardens, craftworkers, palaces, some 200 shrines and 1500 Buddhist temples.

Buddhism came from China a century or so after the Romans left Britain: it opened the stockades of tribal Japan to all things Chinese – art, manners, central administration – and made the Heian era possible. It was also veg-etarian – rice-gruel and two veg for breakfast, and think yourself blessed. There were ways round such virtue, as there always are: an animal was defined as something on four legs, so birds were acceptable, as well as fish. Double-think was applied to make it possible to hunt game – a wild boar, for instance, was redefined as a 'mountain whale'. (Personally, I find this evidence of prevarication a great relief after all that inscrutability. Twisting the rules like that is a sure sign of the presence of the ordinary sort of human being.) But, like it or not, Japan could not afford much meat, with three-quarters of the country mountain and forest and most of the population jammed together on what was left. The Japanese did not eat dairy products – though the amount is going up now, and milch-cows may be heard mooing away in their cowsheds in the midst of cities – so they needed protein from somewhere.

The answer pedals round the streets of Kyoto and other cities every day:

for instead of our milkman with his clatter of bottles, the Japanese have the *tofu*-seller on his bicycle, sounding his horn. It cannot be the most pleasant form of cycling, pushing a large tank of water through the streets, but the fresher *tofu* is, the better – though it will keep for several days in the refrigerator, if the water is changed daily. *Tofu* is beancurd, the beans in question being soya beans: which also make a strongly flavoured protein paste, *miso*, and soy sauce, *shoyu*. A lot of *tofu* comes out of factories nowadays, but Kyoto has some 380 shops still making it in the old way: which, like many old ways with food, has its own functional elegance. The local water is good for *tofu*-making, they say.

Tofu-making is one of those inscrutable processes that gives you no idea at all what the end-product is going to be like: it looks like a brewery at the start, and then turns into a dairy. Golden soya beans arrive at the *tofu*-makers in sacks – not paper bags, or plastic bags, but honest-to-goodness rough hessian sacks – in the back of an old pick-up truck, and are soaked, as if they were going to be fermented into beer. But after eight to twelve hours, they are put into a drum turning above grindstones by courtesy of old leather belts and squeaky cast-iron pulleys of the kind that are outlawed in Britain; and a creamy paste with a greenish tinge oozes down the stone into a wooden tub. This paste is then cooked. It doesn't take long – twenty minutes in about double its volume of boiling water, stirring frequently. Most of the goodness comes out of the beans as a milk, which is separated from the mush by pouring it – ladle by ladle – through a sack. (The remains of the beans themselves can be cooked for humans, but they are usually fed to pigs.)

You can drink the soya milk, or coagulate it to make beancurd. The Chinese use gypsum as a coagulant; the traditional Japanese chemical is *nigari*, which is mostly magnesium chloride and produces a slightly different taste. The coagulant has to be added while the milk is around 70°C (160°F). For a uniform texture it needs to be spread evenly through the milk, but too much stirring makes the texture granular instead of smooth. Covered and kept warm, the milk takes little more than five minutes to set into something like junket. This is the most delicate form of beancurd, which they sell as *kofu*, 'silken beancurd', to be added to soups and eaten half-liquid with various flavourings, particularly as a summer dish. Pressed, *kofu* becomes the coarser-textured but more useful *tofu*, 'cotton beancurd'. The mould is a box with holes in it, lined with cloth; and the beancurd is pressed for ten minutes or so, according to the texture the maker is trying to achieve, with a wooden board and a stone weight that looks as if it belongs to a Japanese garden rather than a *tofu*-maker.

Japan: Salmon Stew page 183

The process is like a kind of vegetable cheese-making – wishy-washy to start with, and a transformation at the end. But, even pressed, large chunks of beancurd are difficult to handle, so the *tofu* is turned out into tanks of water and sliced carefully into blocks, which waft gently to the bottom, where they look like square white stones in the clear, cold water. The beauty is important in Japan: but *tofu* also has half the protein of meat, at a fraction of the price – and a fraction of the taste.

*Tofu* can be bought in Britain from Chinese or Japanese grocers in various forms, including kits for instant *tofu*, which work well. Or it can be made at home by a suitably modified version of the process described above. To one cup of dried beans allow about eight cups of water and one heaped teaspoon of a coagulant, such as calcium sulphate. It is said that lemon juice will also work as a coagulant, but takes some hours.

*Tofu* is not a flavour that fits in with traditional British taste. It can be called fresh, vegetabley and a little sour, but the overriding impression is of blandness with a blancmange-like texture. It does not need to be cooked, and the taste does not change much when it is. However, by pressing some of the liquid out in a cloth or under a weight, *tofu* can be encouraged to reabsorb more interesting flavours in a marinade. Smoked *tofu* is more interesting still, if you can find it. Fried *tofu* we will come to later.

*Miso*, by contrast, is in a yeast-extract class of flavour: it is made from a mixture of soya beans, salt and grain, fermented for a few days and aged – perhaps for years, for it keeps indefinitely. *Miso* is a paste that comes in three varieties of increasing strength and age: *kome*, light: *mugi*, medium; and *hacho*, dark. It came from China in the first place, but dropped out of use there, and survived in Japan. *Shoyu*, soy sauce, may be light or dark. The light is less full-flavoured than the dark, and interferes less with the colour of the dish. Otherwise, the difference is not critically different in character.

Another standard Japanese ingredient is a stock, *dashi*. It is made of *kat-suoboshi* (flakes of dried bonito) and *kombu* (like *nori* and *hijiki*, a seaweed) simmered in water. There is an instant version in powder form which is rather better than the general run of stock cubes. Though a fish stock, it is rather meaty tasting, and chicken stock is quite a good substitute.

For *miso* soup, which is part of the Japanese hearty breakfast, vegetables are simmered in *dashi*. Towards the end of cooking, *miso* and soy sauce are added and then little cubes of *tofu* are plopped in. *Tofu* goes tough when it is overcooked, so the soup is just brought back to the boil and served.

*Tofu* may also be simmered in stock or just chilled in cold water and in

England: Roast Beef with Horseradish Sauce and Yorkshire Pudding page 188 either case served with soy sauce and garnishes such as *daikon* (white radish, like the sort they eat in Munich), *nori, katsuobushi,* ginger and spring onions. (The spring onions are very small and are grown in the dark so that they are yellow; the same thing is done in China with chives.) The hot dish is *Yudofu,* the cold *Hiyayakko.* For *Yudofu* a dash of *mirin* may be added to the soy sauce. *Mirin* is the sort of sweet wine that does not tempt the cook to have nips. I cannot think of any sort of sweet sherry that would fail to substitute, except possibly a good one.

*Meoto-daki* is deep-fried or grilled *tofu,* simmered in *dashi* with *sake* and soy sauce, and garnished with *sansho* leaves – leaves of the Chinese Prickly Ash. In Britain you will have to substitute some other sort of leaf, but *sansho* powder is available. It is lemony and quite unusual in fragrance; I have yet to make up my mind whether it is very useful, or very artificial.

# MATSUZAKA AND TOKYO

*'Apparently, the Americans in America keep to the right in walking, so that they told us also to keep to the right, with the result that our streets are in confusion even today.'*
Kenichi Yoshida

Twice, the course of Japanese history has been changed by the United States. The second occasion is written into the chronicles in ash; the first was a cultural explosion. Not a shot was fired in anger by the American squadron that put into Uraga bay in 1853 – but the Black Ships, as the Japanese called them, were a display of force and superior technology combined. They brought about a crisis of self-doubt and a persistent gale of fascination with the Western world, so strong that very important people proposed that their country should scrap its own language in favour of English; more, there was even a suggestion that Japanese women should be scrapped, in favour of Westerners who might increase the stature of the race. People wore bowler hats above their Japanese costumes; and desired sewing machines and rifles.

The Black Ships came to open a door which had been closed for two centuries. The military clans which had been the basis of Japanese society in the beginning had re-emerged with the weakening of the civilisation of Heian, and a long period of civil wars followed. Christian missionaries from the West were an additional focus of trouble, political as well as spiritual.

The wars between the clans were like a cat-fight in a straitjacket: no hope of keeping them apart, but they might be prevented from damaging each other if someone could pull the strings tight enough. The Tokugawa Shogunate had left the Emperor in Kyoto and set up a power-base in Edo, the modern Tokyo. A cat-fight in a straitjacket does not easily adjust to changes in the balance of power. The Shogunate adjusted the missionaries with the sword; and in 1640 locked up Japan, with death for anyone who went in or out, apart from a tiny community of Dutch merchants in Nagasaki, and threw away the key.

Behind its walls of isolation, the Shogunate used a police state to reinforce a social order which was like an electronic circuit – every component in its place. It was a Confucian hierarchy. The idea had come from China long before, but it was applied far more rigidly in Japan. Generation upon generation of a life-loving people were taught how to respect the superior, how to conform, how to inform. Malingerers and individualists alike did not survive. 'Those who speak feel the cold air on their lips,' runs one proverb. The hive-like habit of work remains to this day; and many a Japanese betrothed sees nothing unusual in using private detectives to check out the past of his beloved before marriage.

Ironically for the nation that was going to produce the most extraordinary manufacturers and traders of our time, the people right at the bottom of the social sump were the merchants. But however much the ruling aristocracy despised them, they still had their hands on the money. Economic power shifted downwards; when the Black Ships came, it began to assert itself. The old order collapsed, and the walls with it: the Emperor Meiji led his people towards a commercial – and, for a time, a warlike – destiny through a half-century of tumultuous change.

In food, the *naifu* and *fokku* did not replace the chopstick: but the Black Ships brought a new tradition of eating beef – for until then, in Japan even more than in China, cattle were for pulling things, not for eating. Very soon, however, the Japanese had taken the import and adapted it to their own advantage – for that is their way, whether it is a matter of commerce, philosophy or food. It also came to be to the advantage of the cows, which are better looked after than the guests in many a hotel.

Their five-star standard of living includes being fed twice a day with a muesli of six types of food mixed at the right temperature, bottled beer every now and again and a confidential massage service by the farmer and his wife. I am sceptical about the advantages of the beer, but the effect of the massage, which is done with stiff brushes, is plain to see. The fat is distributed through the meat so that a steak is marbled with it in a way I have never seen in Britain – and am not likely to see now that the furies of the anti-fat campaign are abroad. The meat is like white and red lace, or an aerial view of a river delta with white water and a pattern of pink islands. Apart from the richness the fat gives to the flavour, such meat is so tender that it can be cut with chopsticks. The top grade is called *shimo-furi* – 'coated with frost'.

The beef raised near Kobe, not far from Osaka, is celebrated for steaks –

and you can eat roast beef in a reproduction English pub complete with ancient beams, the King's Arms Tavern, Fukiai-ku. However, the Wadakin beef of Matsuzaka (near Nagoya in central Japan) is said to have a slight edge for the making of *Shabu-shabu* – the Japanese version of Mongolian Hotpot.

*Shabu-shabu* is named after the noise of a slice of beef swished about in stock. It is made like its Chinese-Mongolian mutton counterpart (see page 145), with the same fine slicing of the meat when half-frozen. But the stock is rather more robust than Chinese stocks generally are; the noodles are *harusame*, 'spring rain', made from sweet potatoes (*harusame* noodles can be found in Britain, but if you have difficulty getting them cellophane noodles will do instead); there are cubes of *tofu* to go with salad vegetables such as Japanese leeks sliced diagonally, Chinese cabbage and mushrooms; and the dipping sauces are ready prepared – Sesame Sauce and *Pon-zu* Sauce.

The *togorashi* used in the Sesame Sauce looks like pure chilli powder, but it is actually a blend of spices, so it is milder (Seven Spices, another useful peppery flavouring, is a possible substitute). Japanese vinegar is milder and sweeter than British malt – use cider vinegar or wine vinegar slightly diluted with white wine. Middle Eastern *tahina* is a source of ready-ground sesame seed, and proprietary sesame paste is sold for use in Chinese cooking.

# SESAME SAUCE
## TOKYO
### ENOUGH FOR 4 TO 6 PEOPLE

| |
|---|
| **100 g (4 oz) white sesame seed** |
| **250 ml (9 fl oz) cold *dashi*** |
| **4 tablespoons dark (*koikuchi*) soy sauce** |
| **4 teaspoons light (*usukuchi*) soy sauce** |
| **2 teaspoons vinegar** |
| **Garlic, crushed, to taste** |
| ***Togorashi*** |

PREPARATION: Toast the sesame seed lightly in a dry pan. To make this sauce with the authentic texture, grind the seed to a paste in a mortar and mix in the other ingredients. To make it easily, put it all in a blender.

# PON-ZU SAUCE
## TOKYO
### ENOUGH FOR 4 TO 6 PEOPLE

| |
|---|
| **2.5 cm (1 inch) length white radish** |
| **1 chilli (mild, if possible)** |
| **1 spring onion, very finely chopped** |
| **5 tablespoons soy sauce** |
| **Juice of 2 lemons** |

PREPARATION: Peel the radish and make 2 holes in the end. Put pieces of chilli in the holes. Grate the radish with the chilli. (This is a clever ruse to enable you to grate a chilli, which on its own is too floppy.) Add the onion. Mix the soy sauce and lemon juice and put into a serving bowl with the spicy radish and onion mixture.

~~ • ~~

*Shabu-shabu* is only one of the *nabe-mono* – meals cooked at table. *Amiyaki* is a table barbecue on charcoal, with fillet steak coated in sauce before grilling. For *Sukiyaki*, thin slices of beef are cooked in an oiled frying pan with sugar, stock, *sake* and soy added to make a sweet and sour sauce; the accompaniments are vegetables cooked in the same way, rice, *sake* and the bowl of beaten egg into which you dip each mouthful of meat hot from the pan.

The traditional way of eating such meals in a restaurant is in a private room with an attentive waitress. (A lot of Japanese eating-out is men-only/business-meeting/expense-account dining; with the restaurant providing a doggy bag in which to take a morsel of charity home for the wife.) But such places are expensive, and things are changing. Hotpot has even entered the realm of fastish food. City lunch-bars have rows of diners at the counter, each confronting a hotpot of stock, rice, egg, salad and a glass of beer.

The rice wine which accompanies *Sukiyaki* is warmed by standing the jug in hot water for a few minutes, and drunk from tiny bowls with care and timing – raising the bowl elegantly, drinking, savouring, contemplating the empty bowl, smoothly returning it to the table. The flavour of *sake* (whose name possibly comes from Osaka) has a transparency that goes particularly well with the fresh tastes of Japanese food, and which allows it to be drunk at any time of the day, even at breakfast. When a tot is taken by itself, a little salt may be placed on the rim of the bowl. Sweet *sake* which actually tastes sweet, rather than smooth, is for the tourist rather than the connoisseur (so is *Sukiyaki* itself, many Japanese would say). A good *sake* is dry, and shows gold in blue and white china. Mature in less than nine months, it is drunk young;

it would be possible for a good natural *sake* to be kept, but it never is. For fifty years it has been the practice to add spirit during fermentation, a measure introduced to conserve rice-stocks, and this has produced a wine of even more transparent character.

Grape wine has been made in Japan since the seventeenth century, but is not of high quality by Western standards, though French and German grapes have been hybridised with the native. Three million gallons of sugared plonk are made a year but, as in the northern nations of the West, the concentration is on grain rather than grape. Along with plenty of good beer, there is reasonable whisky and *shochu* – a spirit which may acquire something of a *sake*-like taste by being passed through the lees of a *sake* fermentation, but which is basically crude in the manner of aquavit and vodka; and which is served by the tumbler.

When drunk with fish, *sake* is sometimes poured over the fin before serving – an acquired taste, particularly if the fish is *fugu*, the deadly blowfish which requires a specially licensed chef to make it safe for eating and which does claim the life of the occasional intrepid diner. Less lethally bizarre is *Odorigyo*, Dancing Fish, a soup containing small live whitefish.

Japanese houses are different from ours, ruled by another understanding of domestic space. An Englishman's home is his castle, but a Japanese home is bamboo and screens – and you cannot build a castle out of that. There are walls between people, as here – but they are invisible ones of formality, taste, respect, responsibility. Few Westerners penetrate this invisible forest of assumptions (even with a Commando course in that rose-garden of vaguenesses, the British class system); though a few may blunder about in the undergrowth.

But despite their rather uptight social system, on the whole the Japanese seem to be a contented and rather happy people. They are much given to festivals – including nude festivals, but these are not so much for fun as for endurance, since they take place in winter, rather like the British Christmas swim, and contestants wear loin-cloths. A popular festival snack is *Inari-zushi* (named after Inari, the rice-god), which is vinegared rice (*sushi*) stuffed into a beancurd pouch as a convenient means of stuffing it into the mouth. The pouch is *abura-age*, a slab of *tofu* which is fried until the outside toughens. The middle, being less cooked, is easy to open out into a bag.

*Abura-age* is usually bought ready made, and frozen packets of it can be found in this country. To make it at home, put slices of beancurd about as thick as a finger into rather less than their depth of lukewarm oil, and bring the temperature of the oil up to 180°C (350°F) over about eight minutes, turning the slices about two-thirds of the way through. Or you can press the slices of beancurd under a weight to take out some of the moisture, then deep-fry them.

The advantage of *abura-age* over *tofu* is that it does not disintegrate in longer cooking and that it takes a flavour (its own is rather neutral) — a feature which is exploited in *Inari-zushi*. In Japan, the pouches are held down during simmering with a device dignified with the name of *otoshi-buta* — a sort of interior saucepan-lid. Such a gadget would be useful in our kitchens.

# INARI-ZUSHI
## MR SHOZABURO HAYAKAWA, TOKYO
### MAKES 10 TITBITS

| |
|---|
| 5 sheets *abura-age* |
| 200 g (7 oz) *sushi* rice |
| 1 tablespoon soy sauce |
| 1 tablespoon *mirin* or sherry |
| 4 tablespoons sugar |
| Salt |

PREPARATION: Prepare *sushi* rice (see below). Pour boiling water over the *abura-age* to remove the residual oiliness, and cut each long sheet across to make 2 pouches. Mix the soy sauce, *mirin*, sugar and salt and simmer the pouches in the mixture until they have absorbed the flavour and have turned golden brown. Stuff the pouches with *sushi* rice. Eat them cold.

~ • ~

When it comes to rice, the Japanese, like the Chinese, prefer it polished. The main Japanese variety is short-grain, and the object is usually not to leave the grains separate, as with Pakistani and Indian rice, but to cook them to the point at which they have a tendency to stick together without becoming a universal mush (much easier for the chopsticks).

# SUSHI RICE
## MR TADASHI UCHIDA, MIYAKO SUSHI BAR, ASAKUSA,

| |
|---|
| To every 450 g (1 lb) of cooked rice: |
| 125 ml (4 fl oz) vinegar (preferably cider vinegar) |
| 1 tablespoon sugar |
| 2 teaspoons salt |

PREPARATION: Put the rice in a heavy pan and pour in cold water to cover it by about 6 mm ($\frac{1}{4}$ inch). Bring it to the boil, cover the pan and simmer until the rice is done and dry (which with polished rice will be in 15 to 20 minutes). It should be just sticky enough to mould. While the rice is cooking, mix the flavourings.

Turn out the rice into a wide container. Sprinkle the flavouring mixture over the hot rice, stirring it in quickly. The Japanese fan the rice to drive off excess moisture. You could try using a hair-dryer.

*Inari-zushi* is nicknamed 'football *sushi*' by the Americans. But the usual accompaniment for the vinegared rice is raw fish. *Sushi* bars are one of the things in Tokyo that strike with a strange, yet familiar ring: like the *rushawa* – the rush hour – and Chuken Hachiko, a dog commemorated in a statue, like Edinburgh's Greyfriars Bobby, and for the same reason (but the Japanese master for whom the faithful animal waited in vain, fed on scraps from the passers-by, was a soldier in the Second World War).

*Sushi* bars are one of the little pockets of humanity in which Tokyo people hide from Tokyo. They have something of the cheerful atmosphere of a pub, with a proprietor at work behind the counter and lots of glasses of beer in evidence. However, it needs more skill to run a *sushi* bar than a pub. The proprietor may well have a generation of filleting behind his nonchalant catering, and the boys in the backroom have five years of apprenticeship to serve.

The art of *sushi* is the art of the knife, as it is with *sashimi* (raw fish without the rice). The essential quality of the fish for both *sushi* and *sashimi* is a freshness such that there is as yet hardly any fishy taste or fishy smell. Otherwise, most kinds of fish are suitable for eating raw in the Japanese manner – though the firmer-fleshed are easier to handle. An extremely sharp knife is vital, and a thin-bladed one is often an advantage. In the fish-markets, tuna are filleted by three men with something like a samurai sword, one man holding each end of the sword, the third man steadying the enormous fish.

*Tai* (a roseate sea bream), *kohada* (a kind of small shad), carp, abalone and sardine are among other favourite fishes. Even in the middle of preparation, the fish are laid out beautifully. There are as many forms of *sushi* as there are cakes in a baker's (including the odd non-fishy variety with things like egg and avocado), but the most usual one is a fish-*wasabi*-rice sandwich. *Wasabi* grows in mountain streams, a green waterplant that looks like a knobbly spear of asparagus and tastes like horseradish: it is crushed to a paste and dabbed on the underside of a diagonal slice of fish, then covered with a ball of rice moulded to the fish with a few deft movements of the fingers.

At its most gaudy, a plateful of *sushi* looks like a hat prepared by a mad milliner with a side-interest in aquariums; at its best, it is the treasure of the deep made to look like jewels.

# SIMPLE SUSHI
## MR TADASHI UCHIDA, MIYAKO SUSHI BAR, ASAKUSA, TOKYO

| |
|:---:|
| **Very fresh fish** |
| **Ice-water** |
| **Garnish vegetables** |
| **Fresh ginger (or other tangy flavouring, such as a mixture of white radish and lemon zest), grated** |
| **Soy sauce** |
| ***Wasabi* (or horseradish), crushed to a paste** |
| ***Sushi* rice** |

PREPARATION: Fillet the fish (or get the fishmonger to do it for you), making the fillets about 4 cm ($1\frac{1}{2}$ inches) across. Put the fish fillets into ice-water. Prepare some garnish vegetables (anything that can be eaten raw and looks pretty). Put the ginger into one serving bowl and the soy sauce into another.

Dry the fish and slice it diagonally at an angle about 1 cm ($\frac{1}{2}$ inch) thick. Put a dab of *wasabi* paste on a slice of fish, take a thumb-and-forefinger-full of the rice and mould it over the *wasabi*, trying not to handle the fish too much but, nevertheless, to create a shape that has some suggestion of the live fish about it. Accompany the *sushi* with vegetables, soy and ginger.

The more you look at the food of Japan, the more obvious the importance of its appearance becomes. *Tempura* may be translated as 'wearing a crust of batter as a woman wears silk gauze, stimulating the desire of the beholder by the glimpses of the beauty beneath'. *Tempura* provides another whole meal cooked at the table, with (usually) first shrimp, then fish, then vegetables, all in bite-sized pieces, dipped in batter and deep-fried. It is accompanied by a dipping sauce of four parts *dashi* to one of soy sauce, with a splash of *mirin*, sugar to taste and some grated radish.

# HOKKAIDO

*Return of the salmon*

Hokkaido, the north island of Japan, is almost Scandinavian and – like the European Nordic countries – has Russia as a neighbour. The winter is rather less harsh than in Sweden, but with enough snow to host the Winter Olympics. There are forests, hot springs, mountains and lakes. Towns are relatively small and there is much more open space than in the main island of Honshu, which has five times as many people to the square inch. They make spirits and beer in Hokkaido; they had a notable herring fishery; and the salmon come to its rivers, as they do in Sweden. The locals call them *aki aji*, 'the taste of autumn', for that is when salted sides of salmon hang drying in the sun and wind, and the shop-counters are silver and red with whole fish and choice cuts. Every possible part of the salmon is eaten down to the heart, and eaten in many different ways – from slices of raw salmon frozen (*ruibe*) to preserved salmon with rice-malt (*izushi*).

A few well-displayed chrysanthemums are not enough to keep out the cold in this climate. In the fishermen's huts, breakfast may be *chan-chan yaki* style – a whole fish stuffed with light *miso* and laid on top of the cast-iron stove to broil (eaten from the stove-top as well, with chopsticks); or the local stew, *Ishikari-nabe* – substantial, warming and comparatively Western in style. It uses the head, bones and even the tail: and when making a modest version of the stew (one not requiring a whole salmon), a small quantity of such parts should be included to make the dish authentic. If you are using a whole fish, it is scaled and gutted, and filleted by passing a knife from head to tail down each side of the backbone. The fillets are sliced across, fins and all, into chunks 5 to 6 cm (2 to 2½ inches) across, and the backbone-to-tail strip is similarly chopped – along with bony parts of the head. *Shirataki*, 'white waterfall' noodles, are made from *konnyaku*, a gelatinous vegetable starch, cubes of which may be used instead in the making of the broth. Arrowroot or cornflour could be substituted. In Japan, leeks are not much larger than spring onions, so they go into the stew right at the end.

# SALMON STEW
## (Ishikari-nabe)
ISHIKARI, HOKKAIDO

ENOUGH FOR 4 PEOPLE

| |
|---|
| **300 g (11 oz) fresh salmon, including some trimmings** |
| **50 g (2 oz) *shirataki* or 1 tablespoon arrowroot or cornflour** |
| **900 ml (1½ pints) cold water** |
| **2 pieces of *kombu* (seaweed), each 7 cm (3 inches) long** |
| **1 medium onion, thinly sliced** |
| **200 g (7 oz) cabbage heart, cut in bite-sized pieces** |
| **125 ml (4 fl oz) *miso*** |
| **1 teaspoon sugar** |
| **2 young leeks** |
| **½ block of *tofu*, cut into cubes** |
| ***Sansho* powder or black pepper** |
| ***Garnish* (optional)** |
| **Salmon roes** |
| **Soy sauce** |

PREPARATION: Cut the salmon flesh into chunks, and the bones into smaller pieces. If using *shirataki*, scald them in hot water to remove the harsh taste.

Put the water on to boil with the *kombu*, onion, cabbage and *shirataki* (or stir in a paste of arrowroot or cornflour). When the broth comes to the boil, put in the *miso*, sugar, salmon and salmon trimmings. Bring back to the boil, skim, and check the amount of *miso*, adding more to taste, if necessary. Put in the leeks and simmer until the salmon is cooked to your taste. This will probably take 5 minutes or less: the general effect of the stew being one of things only just being cooked. The *tofu* goes in when the stew is virtually ready.

Sprinkle with *sansho* (or pepper) and, if you like, garnish with blobs of salmon roe or other similar roe mixed with a little soy sauce.

~~ • ~~

Hokkaido cooking is relatively robust: but on the whole Japanese cuisine is not very good on strong taste and very strong on good taste. Appearance, for instance, is not a matter of titivating a Peacock Hors-d'oeuvre, like the Chinese: or flourishing the silver leaf, like the Pakistanis: or sprinkling the parsley, like the Europeans. It is a revelation of the ingredients and the season quite in character with Shinto, the oldest religion of Japan, which survives alongside Buddhism and whose essence is simplicity and nature-worship. The cooking of fresh ingredients, bringing out natural flavours and colours, is the artlessness of great art.

The Japanese are ascetic where the Chinese are epicurean. Their traditionally austere country itself promotes a habit of discrimination. Japanese seasons do not ingrow on the summer, which – except for Hokkaido – is a rainy season, hot and wet: but centre more on the clarity of autumn, spring and the cold, dry winters.

Combined with the visual ability of a people who can create a Japanese garden is a sense of time and respose astonishing in a nation whose modern life is on permanent fast wind. They watch the flowering of cherries in the understanding that the blossom will soon be gone; and create sand gardens in a land periodically shaken by earthquakes and volcanoes. It is escapist, perhaps, but in all their activity, they find a moment of peace; in all their pushing, an instant of relaxation. In their crowded, polluted cities they make a garden with a flower, a stone and a twisted tree. In their cooking, they can make us think of essentials – as they have done already, with their influence on *nouvelle cuisine*, with its light sauces, discreet portions and elegant pres-entation. Their good taste is not an imposition, but a social norm, an ideal, a respect for tradition all at the same time: it is aesthetic and practical sim-ultaneously. It introduces seldom-considered dimensions into cooking and eating – a timing which makes the action, as well as its results, a delight; and a sense of appropriateness which brings back the vanishing magic of the seasons. (There is no such thing as a dinner service in Japan – each bowl is chosen to complement the food, or the season.)

The cookery of this formal people turns out to be romantic, even joyful: it imitates the forms of nature; it treats ingredients like poetry, for their associ-ations as much as their tastes and culinary qualities. Because of this, it does not spoil their character. It is a philosophy of cooking that calls for skill, frugality, taste in presentation – not pretty-pretty garnish to hide a multitude of sins, but decency.

Japan and its food are changing. It is not merely that the *sushi* selection now trundles round and round some bars on a conveyor belt: the country continues to gulp down ideas from the West, and more meat, dairy products and rather spicier foods are being eaten. A survey of children's tastes by Kikkoman, the soy sauce manufacturer, included only one distinctively Japanese dish (*norimaki* – *sushi* rice with vegetable, egg, fish or pickles wrapped in *nori* seaweed) in the eight favourites. The rest were: Chinese dumplings; noodles in soup; curry and rice; hamburger; macaroni cheese; spaghetti; and the inevitable pizza. A short order from the global kitchen: but the Japanese have only once been successfully invaded; and perhaps their way of making things their own may yet fling some of the vulgarity of fast food to the winds – as long ago the *kamikaze*, the Wind of the Gods, scattered the invading fleets of Kubilai Khan.

Nothing is perfect, of course: their traditional food may be more beautiful than a hamburger, but you might not enjoy it as much. Nevertheless, the world is wide enough to accommodate both aesthetic eaters and stout eaters. I plan to stay a stout eater, myself: but I will take a touch of simplicity and frugality from Japan, as a matter of good taste.

# THE ENGLISH RECIPES

It probably says something about the British character that, in all the hours of programmes made around the world, the BBC's were the only ones to include a shot of the national flag. British public cooking has often had little to wave a flag for, and much of which to be profoundly ashamed. This state of affairs is now improving at the top end of the market, but not nearly enough lower down, though café dishes like cakes, puddings and fish and chips can be marvellous, some pubs hold out bravely against the microwave, the meal-in-the-bag and the metal keg – and the global kitchen has contributed the excellent value of the Indian restaurant. There have been many unsung heroines of home cooking: and the hideous parsimony of the middle classes is giving place to much more intelligent and adventurous bourgeois food: but most people's long detachment from the land as a result of the early industrial revolution must have done much to depress the standards of city-dwellers in the past; and the mass-distribution and convenience food industries of the present day have done little to raise them. The British do not complain – and often do not know what to complain about: which is a disastrous attitude when it comes to food.

The BBC chose the dishes which were going out across the world to be representative rather than exceptional. Cornish Pasty, Steak and Kidney Pie, some simple cheese dishes and Kedgeree were shown in addition to those transmitted in the composite programme seen in Britain – Breakfast Kidneys, a Roast Beef lunch, and Sherry Trifle. Here are the recipes, as a matter of record. The kidneys are a good dish well suited to other meats as well as breakfast, but their best effect rather depends on the quality of the *demi-glace* (a rich, much-reduced sauce based on bone stock) which is added at the end.

Few people will have such a thing to hand, and a good left-over gravy will do quite well.

# BREAKFAST KIDNEYS
## STON EASTON PARK, SOMERSET
### LARGE HELPINGS FOR 4 PEOPLE

| |
|---|
| **10 lambs' kidneys** |
| **50 g (2 oz) butter** |
| **A glass of sherry** |
| **275 ml ($\frac{1}{2}$ pint) *demi-glace* or gravy** |
| **Salt and pepper** |
| ***Garnish* (optional)** |
| **Parsley, finely chopped** |

PREPARATION: Take the kidneys out of their fat and remove the membrane around them. Cut them in half and cut out the core with a sharp knife.

Melt the butter in a frying pan and fry the kidneys as fast as the butter will allow without burning. After about 3 minutes, when one side is browning, turn them over without piercing them and brown the other side.

Add the sherry, then the gravy and season with salt and pepper. Simmer for a few minutes more to mingle the flavours. Serve with fried bread or toast, and a sprinkling of parsley, if you like.

The key factor in the roast (or, more accurately, bake) is the quality of your butcher. Beef must not only be good but well hung, which means two weeks at least – and a loss of moisture and a tying-up of capital which will make the meat dearer. If you can, pay and be thankful: if you cannot, buy a cheaper cut from a good butcher rather than a more pretentious cut from a poor one. Avoid a joint which is dolled up to look the colour of a petunia and is dripping wet. Roasting is about cooking with dry heat. Wet beef works against this, apart from having a different concentration of flavour. If you find a butcher who hangs his meat properly, love him and cherish him.

There are three stages to roasting beef – searing, cooking and resting. If you choose to do all the searing in the oven, rather than using the method below, you will need to start off at a temperature of about 230°C (450°F, gas mark 8). Cooking temperatures – and, therefore, times – are dependent on the quality of the meat, its size and shape, and the preference of the cook: mine being for 190°C (375°F, gas mark 5) whenever I think the meat will stand it, while another might prefer 170°C (325°F, gas mark 3). The individuality of ovens is another unpredictable factor.

Old wives make Yorkshire pudding well, but also tell tales about it. It is a quite straightforward batter, which likes a certain amount of beating – to the tune of about five minutes or more by hand. Given that and a little resting, how and when you mix it is up to you ( but you may like to add a pinch of nutmeg). The method described below is for an electric mixer: making by hand, it is easier to start off by mixing the flour to a paste with a little liquid. A cool batter should go straight into a hot pan.

# ROAST BEEF WITH HORSERADISH SAUCE AND YORKSHIRE PUDDING

ANNE EDMONDSON, AYNSOME MANOR HOTEL, CARTMEL, LAKE DISTRICT

ENOUGH FOR 4 PEOPLE

| |
|---|
| Beef dripping or lard |
| Sirloin of beef, boned and rolled |
| Salt and pepper |
| *Yorkshire Pudding* |
| 275 ml ($\frac{1}{2}$ pint) milk or milk and water |
| 1 egg |
| A good pinch of salt |
| 100 g (4 oz) strong flour |
| *Horseradish Sauce* |
| 2 tablespoons finely grated horseradish root |
| 150 ml ($\frac{1}{4}$ pint) double cream |
| Salt |
| Sugar |
| Juice of half a lemon |

PREPARATION: Preheat the oven to 180°C (350°F, gas mark 4). Put into the roasting tin enough fat to cover the bottom well, and heat it almost to smoking point on top of the cooker. Sear the meat well on all sides, and ends. Sprinkle with salt and black pepper and put into the hot oven for 15 minutes to complete the sealing.

Baste the meat now, and a couple of times more during cooking. Turn the heat down to 170°C (250°F, gas mark 3). Cook for about 15 minutes per 450 g (1 lb) more for rare, good beef. At the end, let the joint rest in a warm place while the Yorkshire pudding cooks.

For Yorkshire Pudding, whisk the milk and egg together and season the mixture with salt. Whisk in the flour a little at a time, to make a pouring batter. Rest it overnight in the fridge. Put the dripping and juices from the roasting tin into your pudding tin, enough to cover the bottom well, and let it heat in the oven during the last 20 minutes of roasting. While you rest the joint, cook the pudding until it is risen and brown – for about 20 minutes at 180–200°C (350–400°F, gas mark 4–6).

To be impartial, horseradish should be grated across the root, since the hottest flavours lie below the skin. Whip the cream and fold in grated horseradish, salt, sugar and lemon juice to taste. It is worth the trouble.

This sherry trifle is a commercially inspired recipe which I would much prefer to make in another way myself, since I am not a supporter of the jelly school of trifle-making. I give the recipe as it was made, but would be inclined to separate the juice from the fruit salad, mix it with the alcohol and soak the sponge in it before adding the fruit itself. This gives an opportunity of adjusting the sweetness – for the need of sugar goes up with the amount of alcohol, which is why many more generous recipes streak the cake with jam. Making a commercial jelly with less than the recommended quantity of water, as here, makes the jelly rather solid. I would prefer to improve the flavour without strengthening the texture, by substituting fruit juice and/or wine for some of the water.

# ENGLISH SHERRY TRIFLE

## THE FORMER MIDLAND HOTEL, MANCHESTER

### ENOUGH FOR 8 PEOPLE

| |
|---|
| Jelly cubes to make 1 litre (1¾ pints) of fruit jelly |
| A mixture of fruits for fruit salad |
| 100 g (4 oz) sponge cake, cut into 5 cm (2 inch) pieces |
| A glass of medium or sweet sherry |
| *Custard* |
| 570 ml (1 pint) milk |
| 50 g (2 oz) caster sugar |
| A few drops of vanilla essence |
| 4 egg yolks |
| 25 g (1 oz) cornflour, blended with a little cold milk |
| 570 ml (1 pint) whipping cream |
| *Decoration* |
| Strawberries or other fresh fruit |
| Angelica |

PREPARATION: Make the jelly using about 275 ml (½ pint) less water than the instructions specify, and put it to one side to cool. Make a fresh fruit salad, for example of orange, banana, grapes, peaches and cherries. Cut the sponge into 5 cm (2 inch) pieces and put it into the serving bowl. Cover it with fruit salad and sprinkle the sherry over the top (and some brandy, if you like). When the jelly is cool, pour it on top: and leave in a cool place to set.

For the custard, put the milk to heat in a saucepan while you whisk the sugar, vanilla essence and egg yolks together in a bowl until the sugar has dissolved. Whisk the cornflour blend into the hot milk, stirring well and continuing to heat until the mixture thickens. Let the mix come well off the boil before whisking it into the egg mixture in a thin stream. Leave in a cool place to set.

When the jelly will support the custard, and the custard is cool, whip the cream till stiff and fold most of it into the custard. Pour the custard on top of the jelly, and decorate with fresh fruit, whipped cream sweetened and piped in patterns, and strips of angelica.

# BIBLIOGRAPHY

Beeton, Isabella, *Mrs Beeton's Book of Household Management*, London, 1861.

Berry, Scyld, *Train to Julia Creek*, London, Hodder and Stoughton, 1985.

*The Best of Swedish Cooking*, Stockholm, LTs Förlag, 1983.

Chen, Pearl Kung and Tien Chi and Tseng, Rose, *Everything You Want to Know about Chinese Cooking*, New York, Barron's, 1983.

Child, Julia, Bertholle, Louisette and Beck, Simone, *Mastering the Art of French Cooking*, New York, Knopf, 1970; London, Michael Joseph, 1977.

Clewlow, Carol, *Hong Kong, Macau and Canton*, Victoria (Australia), Lonely Planet, 1981.

Dallas, E. S., *Kettner's Book of the Table*, new edition, London, Centaur Press, 1968.

Daniel, Glyn, *The First Civilisations*, London, Thames and Hudson, 1968.

Davidson, Alan, *Mediterranean Seafood*, London, Penguin Books, 1972.

Davis, Bernard, *Commodities*, London, Heinemann, 1978.

Delaforce, John, *The Factory House at Oporto*, London, Christie's Wine Publications, 1983.

Eekhof-Stork, Nancy, *The World Atlas of Cheese*, Amsterdam, Spectrum, 1976.

*Fodor's Guide to Germany*, New York and London, Fodor, 1985.

*Fodor's Guide to Japan*, New York and London, Fodor, 1978.

Garland, Sarah, *The Herb and Spice Book*, London, Frances Lincoln, 1979.

Gascoigne, Bamber, *The Great Moghuls*, London, Cape, 1971.

Grigson, Jane, *Fish Cookery*, London, Penguin Books, 1975; *The Observer Guide to European Cookery*, London, Michael Joseph, 1983.

Hallgarten, S. F., *Alsace and Its Wine Gardens*, London, André Deutsch, 1957.

Harlech, Pamela, *Practical Guide to Cooking, Entertaining and Household Management*, London, Macmillan, 1981.

Hartley, Dorothy, *Food in England*, London, Macdonald, 1954.

Heaton, Nell, *Nell Heaton's Cooking Dictionary*, London, John Murray, n.d.

Hewitson, Don, *Enjoying Wine*, London, Elm Tree, 1985.

Hom, Ken, *Ken Hom's Chinese Cooking*, ed. Jenny Stevens, London, BBC Publications, 1984.

Hosain, Attia and Pasricha, Sita, *Cooking the Indian Way*, London, Hamlyn, 1963.

Howe, Robin, *Far Eastern Cookery*, London, The Cookery Book Club, 1972.

Jaffrey, Madhur, *An Invitation to Indian Cooking*, London, Penguin Books, 1976.

Johnston, Mireille, *The Cuisine of the Rose*, London, Penguin Books, 1984.

Károlyi, Alexander, *Hungarian Pageant*, Budapest, George Vajna, n.d.

Kelly, Marie Noëlle, *This Delicious Land*, London, Hutchinson, 1956.

Kirkup, James, *Hong Kong*, London, Dent, 1970.

Lang, George, *The Cuisine of Hungary*, London, Penguin Books, 1985.

Lin, Hsiang Ju and Tsuifeng, *Chinese Gastronony*, new edition, London, Jill Norman and Hobhouse, 1982.

MacMiadhachain, Anna, *Spanish Regional Cookery*, London, Penguin Books, 1976.

McGee, Harold, *On Food and Cooking*, New York, Charles Scribner's Sons, 1984.

McNair-Wilson, Diana, *Hungary*, London, Batsford, 1976.

MacNicol, Fred, *Hungarian Cookery*, London, Allen Lane, 1978.

Marsden, Walter, *The Rhineland*, London, Batsford, 1975.

Montagne, Prosper, *Larousse Gastronomique*, new edition, London, Hamlyn, 1977.

Moorhouse, Geoffrey, *To the Frontier*, London, Hodder and Stoughton, 1984.

Morell, Elizabeth, *A Visitor's Guide to China*, London, Michael Joseph, 1983.

Morris, Jan, *Among the Cities*, London, Viking, 1985.

Ommanney, F. D., *Fragrant Harbour*, London, Hutchinson, 1962.

*Portugal, A Bird's Eye View*, Lisbon, Directorate-General of Diffusion, 1983.

Ridgeway, Judy, *The German Food Book*, Cambridge, Martin Books, 1983.

Root, Waverley, *Food*, New York, Simon and Schuster, 1980.

Scott, David, *The Japanese Cookbook*, London, Barrie and Jenkins, 1978.

Selby, Bettina, *Riding the Mountains Down*, London, Gollancz, 1984.

Shaw, Michael, *History, People and Places in Eastern France*, Bourne End, Buckinghamshire, Spurbooks, 1979.

Singh, Mrs Balbir, *Indian Cookery*, London, Mills and Boon, 1961.

Singh, Dharamjit, *Indian Cookery*, London, Penguin Books, 1970.

Smith, E., *The Compleat Housewife or, Accomplish'd Gentlewoman's Companion*, London, 1727.

Thackeray, Susan, *Living in Portugal*, London, Robert Hale, 1985.

Turner, Anthony and Brown, Christopher, *Burgundy*, London, Batsford, 1977.

Vernon, Tom, *Fat Man on a Bicycle*, London, Michael Joseph, 1981.

Waley, Arthur, *Three Ways of Thought in Ancient China*, London, Allen and Unwin, 1939.

Wason, Betty, *The Art of German Cooking*, London, Allen and Unwin, 1971.

Williams, Professor L. F. Rushbrook, *A Handbook for Travellers in India, Pakistan, Nepal, Bangladesh and Sri Lanka*, London, John Murray, 1975.

Wright, Carol, *Portuguese Food*, London, Dent, 1969.

Yen, Doreen and Feng, Hung, *The Joy of Chinese Cooking*, London, Faber and Faber, 1952.

Yoshida, Kenichi, *Japan is a Circle*, London, Paul Norbury, 1975.

# INDEX